COOK
Malaysian

❧ Lee Sook Ching ❧

Times Books International
Singapore ● Kuala Lumpur

Photography by Andrew Merewether,
assisted by Paul Hilder.

© **1980 Times Books International**
Times Centre, 1 New Industrial Road
Singapore 1953
2nd Floor, Wisma Hong Leong Yamaha,
50 Jalan Pencala, 46050 Petaling Jaya
Selangor

Reprinted February 1982
Reprinted January 1989

Printed by Kim Hup Lee Printing Co Pte Ltd

ISBN 9971 65 546 2

Contents

Seafood

Eggs and Soybean

Vegetables

Soups

Noodles

Desserts and Snacks

Miscellaneous Favourites

Preface

Malaysian food is a delightful and fascinating blend of the best of Malay, Chinese, Indian, Thai and European cuisine. It is therefore not surprising that many recipes in this book are recognizable as non-local dishes adapted to local tastes. Malaysians are, on the whole, very adventurous with food. They love to experiment with food and will constantly keep on trying to improve their recipes in order that their cooking will have that little "something special", be it the addition of some spice or herb or perhaps the subtle blend of an additional flavour. Those who love Malaysian food will agree with me and will find that the different variations of *Rendang* alone will fill a book.

In this book, I have compiled a collection of recipes that I have used over the years. My family and friends have enjoyed these dishes and many who have tried out these recipes have been very successful with them. It is hoped that this book will reach a wider circle of cooks interested in serving their family and friends with good home-cooked food. The recipes have been kept simple for the benefit of those with very limited knowledge and experience of cooking. They will find many basic recipes with simple to follow instructions to guide them to happier and more successful hours spent in the kitchen. With the "useful hints" and a little practice, they should be able to produce some tasty and interesting meals that they can serve with confidence. The experienced cooks may be able to glean some ideas for variety in their meals, or they may be inspired to try improving their recipes to give them the individual touch, so that they too will be able to transform a simple dish into one "fit for the king".

I wish to express my sincere gratitude to all my family and friends who have contributed to my collection of recipes and who have patiently taught me much of what I know now. I would also like to say a special word of thanks to all my friends who went out of their way to help me in so many ways during the photographic sessions. Many thanks also go to Aw Pottery Sdn. Bhd. and C. K. Tang's for the use of their dishes.

To all who use this book, I hope you will enjoy many hours of happy and successful cooking.

Lee Sook Ching

Cooking Terms

Barbecue	-	To cook over hot charcoal or on a revolving spit.
Basting	-	Spooning melted fat, food juices or other liquid (such as marinade) over meat during cooking to keep the meat moist and to improve the flavour.
Blanching	-	Plunging food into boiling water to loosen the skin, to remove strong flavours, to deactivate enzymes or to partially pre-cook.
Blending	-	Mixing a starch or any ground cereal with a liquid to get a smooth cream before adding it to a boiling liquid to prevent it forming lumps.
Braising	-	Cooking in a covered pan in a small quantity of liquid at very low temperature till the food is tender. Braised foods have a better flavour if they are first browned in some fat before braising.
Chopping	-	Cutting into very small pieces. Use a longish knife with a pointed blade like a cook's knife. Hold the knife in your right hand and using your left hand grasp the pointed end of the blade between the thumb and fingers. Hold the pointed end stationary while the blade is moved up and down quickly on the food to chop it.
Coating	-	Covering food to be fried completely and evenly with a thin layer of a liquid like beaten egg or batter, or a dry substance like flour or bread-crumbs, to prevent food from breaking up or to keep food tender and moist.
Dice	-	To cut food into even-sized cubes. First cut food into slices, then strips and finally cut across the strips to get cubes.
Fillet	-	A boneless strip of lean meat or the deboned sides of fish.
Frying a.	-	Dry-frying is frying foods like peanuts, gingelly seeds or grated coconut in a hot frying pan without any oil. The food is stirred continuously to prevent burning until it is browned and cooked.
b.	-	Stir-frying or saute is tossing food in a hot frying pan with only enough oil to lightly coat the food cooked and to prevent sticking.
c.	-	Deep-frying is cooking food immersed in hot oil. The oil should be very hot when the food is put in so that the coating is cooked immediately to seal in the juices. After the food has been put in, turn down the heat to enable the food to cook slowly without burning.
Garnish	-	To decorate a savoury dish before serving. Garnishes should be edible, such as parsley, spring onions, coriander leaves, chillies, tomatoes, hard-boiled eggs, lemon, etc..
Gulai	-	Malay word used extensively in Penang, Johore and Malacca to mean "a curry with gravy".
Kerabu	-	A spicy salad using either dried or fresh prawns.
Laksa	-	A dish of noodles with a spicy soup made with fish or prawns.
Marinade	-	Sauces and seasoning used to flavour and to tenderise meat or fish before cooking.

Pedas	-	Malay word meaning hot, as with chillies.
Scalding	-	Bringing milk to boiling point to retard souring. Pouring boiling water over food to remove the skin, to loosen hair or feathers or to clean the food.
Shredding	-	To cut or grate food into long, thin strips.
Simmering	-	Cooking food in liquid that is below boiling point. The liquid around the food should be just "moving" or "shivering" and not bubbling. During simmering, there is no evaporation of liquid.
Skimming	-	Removing fat or scum from the surface of a liquid. This is done by drawing a metal spoon across the surface.
Steaming	-	Cooking food in the steam from boiling water.
Stewing	-	Slow cooking of food in a seasoned liquid which is kept at simmering point. The liquid is thickened and served with the food as gravy.
Stock	-	A well flavoured liquid made by simmering bones and bits of meat or fish for at least an hour. Strain the liquid to remove bones and skim off all fat before using it as the basis for soups or gravies.
Sambal	-	A spicy mixture of chillies pounded or ground with *blacan* or other spices.
Sambal blacan	-	Fresh chillies pounded with roasted *blacan* in the proportion of 3 to 4 chillies to a piece of *blacan* 2½ x 2½ x ½ cm. Cut the fresh chillies into 1 cm pieces and pound them together with the hot roasted *blacan* just enough to mix the two ingredients together but not to have the chillies too finely pounded. A couple of *daun limau perut* can be pounded with this mixture if desired. Squeeze a little lime juice over the *sambal* just before serving.
Tumis	-	To stir-fry in oil to cook the food and to improve the flavour, e.g. *tumis sambal* before adding liquid and other ingredients to it.

Cutting methods

For acar

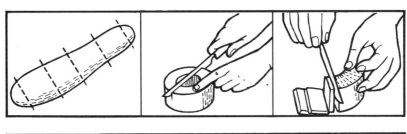

For kerabu

Curls for garnishing

Cooking Hints

1. Meats can be cleaned and prepared ready for use, i.e. minced, sliced or cut up as required, packed into plastic boxes in portions sufficient for a meal, labelled and kept in the freezer till required.

2. Prawns and fish can also be shelled, cleaned and cut up as required before packing and putting in the freezer to freeze for 2 to 3 weeks till required.

3. Grated coconut can be stored in the freezer. Take it out at least 1 hour before it is required to give it time to thaw.

4. Ground curry or *sambal* ingredients, including *sambal blacan,* can be prepared in bulk and stored in the freezer to be used as required. For *sambal blacan,* it is better to freeze it without the lime juice, which can be added just before serving.

5. Shallots and garlic can be chopped or sliced in advance, kept in plastic boxes with tight-fitting lids to keep the smell in, and stored in the refrigerator for use during the week.

6. To fry crispy brown shallots, make sure the shallots are sliced evenly to ensure even cooking. For 1 cup sliced shallots, heat up about 1 cup oil in a frying pan. When the oil is smoking hot, add in the shallots and stir them in the hot oil till they are just beginning to brown. Turn down the heat and continue stirring till the shallots are a light golden-brown. Remove them from the oil with a draining spoon, drain them on kitchen paper and when they are cold, store them in an air-tight jar.

7. To fry browned garlic, chop the skinned garlic till very fine. For each spoonful of chopped garlic, heat up 1 tablespoon oil in a frying pan. When the oil is hot, add in the prepared garlic and stir it in the hot oil till it begins to brown around the sides. Turn off the heat altogether or remove the pan from the fire and continue stirring the garlic in the oil till they are evenly browned. Collect the browned garlic to one side of the pan and scoop them up into a dish to cool. When cool, store them in an air-tight jar with or without the oil, as desired.

8. To roast peanuts, rub peanuts in a tea towel or between two sheets of kitchen tissue to remove dust and dirt. Put the peanuts into a *kwali* or a frying pan and dry-fry over low heat for 20 to 25 minutes, stirring all the time till the peanuts are evenly browned and cooked. Turn the browned peanuts into a colander, and with the help of a pair of cotton gloves to protect the fingers from getting burnt, rub the peanuts against the colander to remove the skin. Shake the colander and the skin can be blown away quite easily. When the peanuts are cold, store them in an air-tight container.

9. To ground peanuts — the electric blender does this very quickly. To prevent peanuts getting too finely ground, switch on the blender and off immediately and you will get ground peanuts and not powdered peanuts.

10. To grind curry ingredients and *sambal* — the electric blender does this quickly too. Cut up the ingredients roughly before putting them in the blender. Candlenut needs

thin slicing before it will blend well. Add water as instructed and blend the ingredients to the fineness required. Always remember that blended sambals require a longer time to *tumis* so that the water in the sambal will be evaporated.

11. To fry or *tumis* curry or *sambal* ingredients — heat up 5 to 6 tablespoons of oil for every cup of ground ingredients. Fry the ground ingredients in the hot oil with ½ teaspoon salt over a low fire, stirring all the time for 5 to 10 minutes till the oil seems to separate from the ground ingredients. This is the stage when curry or *sambal* ingredients are said to be cooked and aromatic.

12. To prepare and clean prawns —
   a. Shell prawns, slit them down the back and de-vein them. Mix 1 tablespoon salt with each pound of prawns and leave them for 10 minutes. Wash them well and drain them. Either use them immediately or pack them in portions and freeze them at once.
   b. When prawns are to be cooked with their shells, cut off part of the head from where the beak begins. With the help of the sharp beak just cut off, dig into the cut head, just under the shell and remove the gritty sac. Trim off the legs and rub them all over with salt. After 10 minutes, wash away the salt, drain them and they are ready for cooking or freezing.
   c. Freshwater prawns should have part of the head from where the beak begins cut off, then split each prawn in two lengthwise. Remove the gritty sac in the head and the vein along the back. Wash the prawns, drain well before seasoning them for cooking. Freshwater prawns should be eaten as fresh as possible and should not be kept for more than 3 days in the freezer.

13. To use curry powder. Always blend curry powder into a paste with water before you fry or *tumis* it.

14. To make special salt , fry together salt and five-spiced powder for several minutes.

Cooking Rice

(For 1 cup of rice, use 1 cup water)

With the introduction of the electric rice cooker into most homes, boiling rice has become a very simple matter. One has only to follow the instructions that come with the rice cooker and fluffy rice is the result. However, for those without rice cookers, here are a few points to remember. The secret lies in the correct amount of water added to the rice before boiling and in the very slow cooking for the last 15 minutes after the water has been absorbed. The amount of water needed depends partly on the type of rice available, so get to know your rice . After washing the rice, drain away the water and add in the measured amount of water. Cover the pan and allow the rice to cook till all the water is absorbed. If the rice looks uncooked at this stage, it needs more water, so add ¼ or ½ cup more water and allow it to cook again till the water is absorbed. When the water is absorbed, the rice grains have all burst but they do not look fluffy. It is then necessary to turn the fire down to as low as possible, or if an electric hot plate is being used, turn it off. Keep the pan covered and allow the rice to finish cooking and dry out for the last 15 minutes. When dishing up rice for serving, loosen the rice first with a shallow rice ladle so that the rice becomes loose, fluffy grains.

Pandan Juice

Mention must be made of 2 ingredients that are the basic ingredients for many local cakes and which are not always readily available. The ingredients are *pandan* juice and damp ground rice or damp rice flour. Although *Pandan* Essence is available in some countries, it is still not readily available. Moreover, the essence, while giving the flavour, does not give the colour and so artificial colouring has to be used. If *pandan* leaves are available, they should be used as their flavour and colour cannot be matched by any artificial flavours and colours. To get *pandan* juice, wash 10 to 12 *pandan* leaves (the older ones are better), pile about 5 or 6 leaves together and pound them till they are all fibrous-looking. Wrap the pounded *pandan* leaves in a damp piece of calico and squeeze out the juice. This *pandan* juice colours the food and at the same time gives it the peculiar *pandan* flavour.

Damp Rice Flour

To get damp rice flour, soak washed rice over-night. Grind the soaked rice in an electric blender till it is very fine. Pass the ground rice through a hair-sieve before pouring it into a calico bag. Hang up the bag of ground rice and allow it to drip dry. The damp rice flour in the bag can be weighed out, labelled, packed and then frozen until required.

Extracting Coconut Milk

The easiest method to extract coconut milk is to use a calico bag.

Coconut milk can be extracted from the grated flesh of mature fresh coconuts. To get grated coconut, gently knock the shell of a mature nut all over with the back of a heavy chopper or axe. This helps to loosen the flesh from the hard shell. Then with a hard knock, crack the nut in half and either pry the flesh from the shell with a sharp knife or chop away small pieces of the shell until all is removed. Peel away the brown skin from the white flesh, wash them and then grate them with a coarse grater.

To extract coconut milk, have 2 bowls ready, one of about 1 pint capacity and the other of about 2 pints. Fill the larger bowl with 2 cups water. Fill the rinsed calico bag with about ¼ grated coconut and squeeze out as much thick milk as possible into the small bowl. Then place the whole bag of coconut into the second bowl and knead the bag of coconut in the water to get the second milk. Squeeze the bag of coconut as dry as possible before throwing away the coconut. Repeat with the next lot of coconut and continue till coconut milk has been extracted from all the coconuts. When emptying the coconut from the bag, turn the whole bag inside out so that no coconut sticks to the outside of the bag. Then turn the whole bag back the right way again before filling it with coconut once more. In this way it is possible to get ¾ to 1 cup thick milk from one coconut.

Grated coconut can be frozen and kept till required. To extract milk from frozen coconut, place the frozen grated coconut in an electric blender with 2 cups hot water and blend for 30 seconds. Pour portions of the blended mixture into a rinsed calico bag and squeeze out as much milk as possible.

Desiccated coconut from a tin can be soaked in 3 cups hot water for at least 15 minutes, or until mixture cools.

Frozen coconut cream and tinned coconut cream are available from supermarkets.

Weights and Measures

Accuracy in measuring and weighing ingredients is essential for successful cooking. This is particularly so in the light desserts and cakes where incorrect amounts of ingredients could spoil the dish altogether. It is fully realised that most countries have converted or are converting to the metric system. This being the case, all recipes should be given in metric. However, it must be realised that it is going to take housewives a very long time to think automatically in metric, neither are they going to throw away all their kitchen scales and measuring jugs to buy new ones, nor are they going to sit down to convert all their old favourite recipes into the new system. After much thought and careful consideration, it has been decided that the simplest solution will be to use measures rather than weights. It has often been said that measures are not as accurate as weights, but with a little care, one is just as accurate as the other.

The measures used are the American standard measuring cups and spoons. The measuring cups are easily obtainable in sets of 4 — 1 cup, ½ cup, ⅓ cup and ¼ cup. The cup is equivalent to 8 ounces. The spoons are also easily available in sets of 4 — 1 tablespoon, 1 teaspoon, ½ teaspoon and ¼ teaspoon. It must be remembered that when measuring dry ingredients, always fill the measure to overflowing and without shaking it, level off with the straight edge of a knife.

Table for use of cups and tablespoons

Food	weight of 1 cup	No. of tabsp. to 1 oz.
flour	4 oz. (113 g)	4 tabsp.
granulated sugar	8 oz. (227 g)	2 tabsp.
castor sugar	7 oz. (198 g)	2 tabsp.
cornflour	4 oz. (113 g)	2 tabsp.
rice	8 oz. (227 g)	

Liquid Measure — Equivalents

1 teaspoon	— ⅓ tablespoon
1 tablespoon	— 3 teaspoons
2 tablespoons	— 1 oz (28g)
4 tablespoons	— ¼ cup
8 tablespoons	— ½ cup
1 cup	— ½ pint or 8 fl. oz. (¼ litre)

Basic Equipment

Grater

Knives

kitchen knife
table knife
potato peeler
vegetable knife

Ladles & Spoons

draining spoon
fish slice
rice ladle
soup spoon
tablespoon
teaspoon
wire ladle
wooden spoon

Masher

Moulds

aluminium custard mould
kueh rose mould
roti jala mould
tophat mould

Sieves

wire sieve
hair sieve
sifter

Scraper

Shredder

Pastry equipment

pastry cutter
pastry pinch
pastry roller
rolling pin
tart cutter

Pots & Pans

aluminium steamer
bamboo steamer
belanga
clay pot
frying pan
kwali (wok)
saucepan
steamboat

Pineapple tart cutter

Wire sieve

Fish slice

Masher

Sifter

Hair sieve

There is no spectacle on earth more appealing than that of a beautiful woman in the act of cooking dinner for someone she loves.

Thomas Wolfe

Rice

Savoury Rice

Preparation: 15-20 mins.
Cooking   : 30 mins.
Serves   : 4-6

10 ounces (300 g) fillet steak
1 inch (2½ cm) piece of ginger
2 teaspoons tapioca flour
2 teaspoons soy sauce
5 tablespoons oil
shake of pepper
6-8 shallots, sliced
1 pound (450 g) rice
1 teaspoon salt
2-3 teaspoons chopped spring onion

Slice steak thinly, cutting across the grain. Marinate in a mixture of ginger juice extracted from pounded ginger, tapioca flour, soy sauce, 1 tablespoon oil and pepper.

Heat remaining oil in a frying pan and brown the shallots. Keep browned shallots for garnishing. Add seasoned steak to hot oil and stir-fry for 1 minute. Remove the pan from heat.

Wash rice and boil it with 1 teaspoon salt added to the water. When rice is almost cooked and water is all absorbed, add in the lightly cooked steak. Cover pan tightly and allow rice to finish cooking on very low heat.

When rice is well cooked, loosen the grains with chopsticks or a fork and at the same time mix the meat with the rice. Season rice to taste and serve it garnished with browned shallots and spring onion.

Savoury Glutinous Rice

Preparation: 25 mins.
Cooking   : 1 hr.
Serves   : 6-8

1 pound (450 g) glutinous rice
2 tablespoons dried prawns
4 ounces (100 g) dried oysters
4 Chinese mushrooms
8 ounces (225 g) prawns
4 tablespoons oil
10-12 shallots, sliced
2 tablespoons soy sauce
1 tablespoon oyster sauce
1 teaspoon sesame oil
½ teaspoon salt
2-3 teaspoons chopped spring onion

Soak rice overnight. Rinse and drain well. Wash the following and soak separately for 10 minutes: dried prawns, dried oysters and Chinese mushrooms. Shell and devein fresh prawns. Dice fresh prawns, dried prawns, dried oysters and mushrooms.

Heat oil and brown shallots. Set aside. In the same oil, fry fresh prawns, dried prawns, dried oysters and mushrooms for 2 minutes. Add rice and toss to mix thoroughly.

Mix together soy sauce, oyster sauce, sesame oil, salt and ½ cup water and add this mixture gradually to the fried ingredients. Stir to mix, cover and cook on very low heat till rice is cooked. Turn rice and stir every 10 minutes to prevent burning. Garnish with spring onion and browned shallots.

Lotus Leaf Rice (top)
Loh Mai Kai (bottom)

Recipe: p. 7

3

Pork Broth

Recipe: p. 12

clockwise — Nasi Kunyit, Acar Timun, Rendang   *Recipes: pp. 11, 71, 25*

Nasi Biryani

Recipe p. 11

Loh Mai Kai (Chicken in Glutinous Rice)

Preparation: 20-25 mins.
Cooking   : 50-60 mins.
Serves   : 4-6

1 pound (450 g) glutinous rice
5 Chinese mushrooms
½ chicken
2 tablespoons soy sauce
½ teaspoon black soy sauce
2 tablespoons oyster sauce
2 teaspoons sesame oil
1 tablespoon sugar
¼ teaspoon pepper
7 tablespoons oil
4 ounces (100 g) roast pork *(char siew)*
8 ounces (225 g) pork
1 tablespoon cornflour
½ teaspoon salt
2-3 teaspoons chopped coriander leaves

Soak rice overnight. Rinse and drain well. Wash and soak mushrooms. When soft, cut into halves. Cut chicken into ½ inch (1 cm) pieces. Season with ½ tablespoon soy sauce, 1 tablespoon oyster sauce, 1 teaspoon sesame oil and 1 teaspoon sugar. Slice roast pork into 10 pieces. Dice pork into ½ inch (1 cm) cubes and season with ½ tablespoon soy sauce, ½ teaspoon black soy sauce, 1 tablespoon oyster sauce, 1 teaspoon sesame oil, the remaining sugar and a good shake of pepper.

Heat 2 tablespoons oil and fry chicken until it is cooked and all the gravy is absorbed. Remove and set aside.

Heat another 2 tablespoons oil, add pork and toss for 1 minute. Add mushrooms and ¼ cup water, then cover and simmer for 10 minutes. Blend cornflour with ¼ cup water, and thicken gravy with this mixture when pork is cooked. Set aside.

Mix drained rice with 3 tablespoons oil, 1 tablespoon soy sauce, ½ tablespoon sugar and ½ teaspoon salt.

Divide chicken, roast pork, the fried pork and mushrooms into 10 equal portions. Place a portion of each into an aluminium bowl. Divide rice into 10 portions and cover the ingredients of each bowl with 1 portion of rice. Bowls should be only half full.

Steam bowls of rice over boiling water for about 30 minutes or till rice is well-cooked. Serve by turning each bowl of rice on to a serving dish so that the meat is on top. Garnish with chopped coriander leaves.

Note: If desired, portions can be wrapped up in lotus leaves and steamed as Lotus Leaf Rice.

Lontong (Rice in Banana Leaves)

Preparation: 10 mins.
Cooking   : 2-3 hrs.
Serves   : 4

2 cups rice
banana leaves *or* **aluminium foil**

Soften banana leaves by scalding them. Clean and dry them. Wash rice and drain.

Wrap rice in banana leaves loosely to get cylindrical packets about 6 inches (15 cm) long and about 1-2 inches (2½-5 cm) in diameter. Fasten with toothpicks or staple together. Alternatively, wrap rice in aluminium foil. Remember that there must be room in the packets for the rice to expand while cooking. The packets should be no more than three quarters full. Place rice packets in a large pan filled with water and boil for 2-3 hours. If necessary, add more water to the pan.

Cool, slice into ¼ inch (½ cm) sections and serve.

Note: Lontong is usually served with *Masak Lodeh* (p. 71) and *Sambal Kelapa* (p. 75), or with *Gado-Gado* (p. 70).

Fried Rice

Preparation: 10 mins.
Cooking   : 10 mins.
Serves   : 4-6

½ cup prawns
½ cup *char siew*
1 pair Chinese sausages
2 eggs
1 teaspoon salt
shake of pepper
4 tablespoons oil
½ cup green peas
4 shallots, sliced
2 teaspoons soy sauce
3 cups cooked rice
2-3 teaspoons chopped spring onion

Shell and devein prawns. Dice prawns, *char siew* and Chinese sausages. Beat eggs with ¼ teaspoon salt and a shake of pepper.

Heat 2 tablespoons oil and scramble eggs till set. Remove. Heat another 2 tablespoons oil, brown shallots, then fry prawns, sausages and *char siew* together for 1 minute. Add green peas, ½ teaspoon salt and soy sauce and stir-fry for another minute.

Add loosened cooked rice and stir-fry all together for 5 minutes. Mix in scrambled egg. Season to taste and serve garnished with spring onion.

Rice with Long Beans

Preparation: 20 mins.
Cooking   : 30 mins.
Serves   : 4-6

½ pound (225 g) pork
2 tablespoons dried prawns
3 tablespoons oil
6-8 shallots, sliced
2 teaspoons salt
2-3 teaspoons soy sauce
10-12 long beans, diced
1 pound (450 g) rice
shake of pepper

Wash and mince pork. Wash and cut dried prawns.

Heat 3 tablespoons oil and brown the shallots. Set aside for garnishing. In the same oil, stir-fry minced pork and dried prawns. Add ½ teaspoon salt and 1 teaspoon soy sauce with 2-3 tablespoons water. Cook for about 5 minutes. Add diced long beans. Mix it thoroughly with meat. Remove all ingredients and set aside.

Wash rice and boil with 1 teaspoon salt. When rice is dry and almost cooked, add cooked ingredients and allow rice to finish cooking over very low heat.

When rice is cooked, stir well to mix the ingredients. Season to taste and serve garnished with browned shallots and with *sambal blacan,* if desired.

Chicken Rice — Hainanese Style

Preparation: 30 mins.
Cooking   : 1 hr.
Serves   : 6-8

1 chicken, about 3½-4½ pounds (1½-2 kg) in weight
2 teaspoons sesame oil
1 teaspoon soy sauce
1 chicken bouillon cube
5 cloves garlic
1 pound (450 g) rice
1 chicken bouillon cube
2 tablespoons oil
2 teaspoons salt
2 teaspoons sugar
* 10 chillies
* 2 inch (5 cm) piece ginger, ground/chopped
* 1 tablespoon tomato ketchup
* 1 tablespoon vinegar
* to be mixed together, for chilli sauce

In a pan big enough to hold the whole chicken, boil enough water to just cover the chicken. When the water boils, put in the chicken, turn down heat to low and cook the chicken covered for 10 minutes. Turn off heat and leave the chicken to continue cooking in the water for another 40 minutes. Remove chicken and put it into a basin of cold water for 15 minutes. Hang chicken up to dry and then brush it over with 1 teaspoon sesame oil mixed with 1 teaspoon soy sauce. Cut off the legs, wing tips and neck and put them back to boil in stock.

Chop 4 cloves of garlic finely. Wash rice and drain it.

Heat 1 tablespoon oil and brown the garlic. Add rice, stir-fry for 1 minute, then add enough chicken stock to cook it. Add bouillon cube, 1 teaspoon salt, 1 teaspoon sugar and 1 teaspoon sesame oil and cook until liquid is absorbed and rice is cooked.

Serve rice with chicken cut into inch-wide (2½ cm) pieces and garnished with cucumber, tomatoes and spring onion. The following chilli sauce is a necessary accompaniment.

Chilli Sauce for Chicken Rice

Pound together the chillies, 1 clove garlic and ginger until very fine. Heat 1 tablespoon oil and fry pounded ingredients. Add 1 teaspoon salt, 1 teaspoon sugar, tomato ketchup, vinegar, 1 teaspoon sesame oil and 4 tablespoon stock. When boiled, season the sauce well, cool it and serve with chicken.

Note: Extra stock can be served as soup. Add seasoning and any vegetable like cabbage, spinach or lettuce.

Salt Fish Rice

Preparation: 15-20 mins.
Cooking   : 30 mins.
Serves   : 4-6

½ pound (225 g) pork
2 tablespoons dried prawns
3 ounces (75 g) salt fish
3 tablespoons oil
6 shallots
1 pound (450 g) rice
1 teaspoon salt
2-3 teaspoons chopped spring onion
shake of pepper

Wash and mince pork, cut dried prawns and dice salt fish.

Heat 3 tablespoons oil and brown shallots. Set aside for garnishing. In the same oil, fry salt fish till slightly brown. Remove. Fry pork and dried prawns till well cooked. Remove

and mix with salt fish.

Wash and boil rice with ½ teaspoon salt. When rice is almost dry, add salt fish and meat mixture and allow rice to finish cooking on very low heat.

When rice is cooked, stir to mix all ingredients thoroughly. Season to taste and serve garnished with spring onion and browned shallots.

Note: Any kind of salt fish (with few bones) can be used. Long beans, cut into ¼ in(½ cm) sections may be added, if desired. Dish may be served with *sambal blacan.*

9

Chicken Rice in Clay Pot

Preparation: 15-20 mins.
Cooking   : 30 mins.
Serves   : 4-6

½ chicken, about 2 pounds (900 g) in weight
5 Chinese mushrooms
½ inch (1 cm) piece of ginger
1 teaspoon salt
1 tablespoon soy sauce
3 tablespoons oil
4 shallots, sliced
1 pound (450 g) rice
1 pair Chinese sausages
2-3 teaspoons chopped spring onion

Clean and cut chicken into small pieces. Soak mushrooms till soft, then wash and cut into halves or quarters. Pound ginger and squeeze for juice. Season chicken pieces with ginger juice, ½ teaspoon salt and soy sauce.

Heat the oil and brown shallots. Add chicken and mushrooms and fry till chicken pieces are firm.

Wash rice, add ½ teaspoon salt and put it on to boil in a clay pot. When rice is cooked and almost dry, add the fried ingredients together with the whole sausages, placing the sausages on top. Cover and allow rice to finish cooking on very low heat. A rice cooker may be used instead of a clay pot.

When rice is cooked, remove sausages and slice diagonally into ½ inch sections. Return sliced sausages to rice and stir to mix all ingredients thoroughly. Season to taste and serve rice garnished with spring onion.

Nasi Lemak (Coconut Milk Rice)

Preparation: 10 mins.
Cooking   : 30-40 mins.
Serves   : 4-6

1 coconut, grated
1 pound (450 g) rice
1 teaspoon salt
2 *pandan* leaves

Extract 3 cups coconut milk from grated coconut.

Wash rice and drain it. Put rice into a steamer, add salt, *pandan* leaves and santan and steam over boiling water for 30 minutes. Stir rice after 30 minutes, then test if it is cooked. If not, steam for another 10 minutes or until cooked. Remove *pandan* leaves and loosen rice with a fork.

Note: Nasi Lemak can be served with Sambal Ikan Bilis (p. 48) Fried Assam Prawns (p. 57), Rendang (p. 25), Fried Peanuts , Fried Fish with Curry Powder (p. 46), Boiled Eggs, and cucumber.

Nasi Kunyit (Yellow Rice)

Preparation: 20 mins.
Cooking   : 40 mins.
Serves   : 6

1 piece turmeric, 2-3 inches (5-7 cm) in length
1 pound (450 g) *pulut* **or glutinous rice**
1 slice tamarind *(assam gelugor)*
10-15 peppercorns
2 *pandan* **leaves**
½ coconut, grated
1 teaspoon salt

Clean turmeric and pound till fine. Place it in a piece of muslin and tie it up firmly. Wash rice and soak in a bowl of water with the turmeric bag and tamarind slice for at least 3 hours. It is better to soak it overnight. Rinse soaked rice under a running tap and drain it.

Put rice in a steamer with peppercorns and *pandan* leaves and steam over boiling water for 20-30 minutes. While rice is being steamed, extract 1-1½ cups thick coconut milk. Add salt to the coconut milk.

When rice is cooked, dish it into a large bowl and mix it with the thick coconut milk so that the rice grains are loosened. Return rice to the steamer and steam for another 10 minutes. When the rice is well cooked, it is soft, shiny and in loose grains. Serve with chicken curry, beef curry or *rendang*.

Note: Pulut takes a long time to soften. Soaking overnight helps to soften the grains.

Nasi Biryani (Spiced Rice with Chicken)

Preparation: 30-35 mins.
Cooking   : 1 hr.
Serves   : 4-6

1 chicken, about 2 pounds (900 g) in weight
1 clove garlic
2 inch (5 cm) piece ginger
2 chillies
1 tablespoon poppy seeds
10 cashew-nuts
10 almonds
4 tablespoons ghee
5 cloves
2 inch (5 cm) cinnamon stick
1 cup shallots, sliced
2-3 teaspoons salt
1 teaspoon curry powder
½ cup yoghurt
½ coconut, grated
1 pound (450 g) rice

Cut chicken into 4 pieces. Grind together garlic, ginger, chillies, poppy seeds, cashew-nuts and almonds.

Heat ghee and fry cloves, cinnamon and shallots. Add chicken pieces, 1 teaspoon salt, ground ingredients and curry powder. Stir to mix and cook covered for 10 minutes. Add yoghurt and simmer till chicken is tender and mixture is thick.

Extract 1-2 cups coconut milk from coconut. Add coconut milk and 1 teaspoon salt to the washed rice and cook it. When the rice has absorbed all the milk, make a well in the centre and put in the chicken mixture. Cover and allow rice to finish cooking over very low heat.

Serve Nasi Biryani with a *chutney.*

Fish Broth

Preparation: 25 mins.
Cooking   : 1½-1¾ hrs.
Serves   : 4

½ cup rice
2 tablespoons oil
10 ounces (300 g) fillet of pomfret or threadfin
2 teaspoons soy sauce
1 teaspoon sesame oil (optional)
½ teaspoon salt
6 slices ginger, shredded finely
2 teaspoons *tong choy*
3 teaspoons chopped spring onion
2 teaspoons chopped coriander leaves
good shake of pepper
¼ piece rice vermicelli (meehoon)

Wash rice and boil with 2 tablespoons oil and 6 cups water. When it boils, turn down the heat and allow the broth to simmer for 1-1½ hours.

Wash and slice fish thinly. Marinate the slices in a mixture of soy sauce, sesame oil, ¼ teaspoon salt and a good shake of pepper.

Place fish slices, ginger strips and *tong choy* in a large, warmed serving dish. Dish the boiling broth into the serving dish, sprinkle spring onion, coriander and pepper on top and serve at once. The boiling broth will cook the fish slices.

Pork Broth

Preparation: 25 mins.
Cooking   : 2 hrs.
Serves   : 4

½ cup rice
1 tablespoon oil
10 ounces (300 g) pork
2 teaspoons soy sauce
1 teaspoon salt
shake of pepper
2 teaspoons tapioca flour
3 ounces (75 g) pig's liver
1 teaspoon sesame oil
2 teaspoons *tong choy*
2-3 teaspoons chopped spring onion
¼ piece rice vermicelli (meehoon)

Wash rice and put it to boil with 1 tablespoon oil and about 6 cups water. When it boils. turn down the heat and allow broth to simmer for 1-1½ hours.

Wash pork and mince it very finely. Add 1½ teaspoons soy sauce, ½ teaspoon salt, pepper and tapioca flour to minced meat and mix it thoroughly. Shape meat into little meatballs of 1 inch (2½ cm) diameter. Wash and cut liver into very thin slices. Season it with ½ teaspoon salt, ½ teaspoon soy sauce and pepper.

When broth is ready, add meatballs to it and cook for a further 3-4 minutes. When meat is cooked, add liver and as soon as broth boils again, turn off heat. Season broth and add sesame oil if desired. Serve it in a warmed dish and sprinkle *tong choy*, spring onion and pepper on top.

Chicken Broth

Preparation: 30-40 mins.
Cooking   : 2 hrs.
Serves   : 4

½ chicken, about 2 pounds (900 g) in weight
1-2 teaspoons salt
½ cup rice
1 tablespoon oil
6 slices ginger, shredded finely
2-3 teaspoons chopped spring onion
shake of pepper

Clean the chicken. Heat 10 cups water in a big pan and when it boils put in the chicken. Turn the heat to very low and simmer for 30 minutes. Remove the chicken and debone it. Return bones to stock. Cut chicken meat into ½ inch (1 cm) strips and season with ½ teaspoon salt.

Wash the rice and put into stock to cook. When rice is soft, simmer for a few more minutes before turning off heat. If a very soft, thick broth is desired, simmer till rice grains are broken, adding more boiling hot water if necessary, and oil.

When broth is ready to serve, remove the chicken bones and add 1 teaspoon or more salt to it. Place chicken pieces with ginger strips in a large warmed serving dish. Dish hot broth over the chicken, sprinkle spring onion and pepper on top and serve at once.

Note: As an added garnishing for the three types of broth, deep-fry a ¼ piece of dry rice vermicelli *(meehoon)* till light-brown, puffy and crispy. Sprinkle fried vermicelli on top of broth just before serving.

Meat

Char Siew (Chinese Roast Pork)

Preparation: 10 mins.
Cooking   : 25-30 mins.
Serves   : 6

1¼ pounds (560 g) shoulder pork
3 tablespoons fish sauce
3 tablespoons sugar
1 tablespoon rice wine

Cut pork into 1 ½ inch (3 cm) strips. Marinate pork with fish sauce, sugar and rice wine and leave it for at least 2 hours. Turn meat over every 30 minutes.

Heat the grill, put seasoned pork strips into the pan grill slowly for about 15 minutes on each side. Brush seasoning sauce on the pork strips every 5 minutes. (If no grill is available, heat 1 tablespoon oil in a frying pan and fry the strips till cooked and brown).

The seasoning sauce can be cooked in a pan till it is thick and poured over the sliced roast pork before serving.

Yuen Tai (Stewed Pork Shoulder)

Preparation: 20 mins.
Cooking   : 1 ¾-2 hrs.
Serves   : 6-8

1¼ pounds (500 g) pork shoulder or thigh
2 tablespoons oil
1 teaspoon *fah chew*
1½ teaspoons fish sauce
1 tablespoon oyster sauce
1 tablespoon black soy sauce
1 thumb-sized piece rock sugar
1 teaspoon Chinese wine

Clean meat and tie it into a neat roll. Heat 2 cups water in a pan. When water boils put roll of meat in for about 10 minutes, turning constantly so that all parts will be immersed in boiling water for a little while.

Take out partially cooked meat and keep the stock for later use. Heat 2 tablespoons oil in a pan, put in meat and turn it in the oil till it is well coated. Add the stock and the *fah chew*, which has been tied in a piece of muslin, and boil for 10 minutes.

Add the fish sauce and allow meat to simmer slowly for 1 ½ hours. When meat is tender, add the oyster sauce, black soy sauce, rock sugar and Chinese wine. Season to taste and serve the meat whole on a bed of boiled green vegetables, like mustard green or lettuce, on a warmed serving dish.

Note: Fah Chew is a spice obtainable from Chinese medicine shops. *Fah tew siew chow* is a Chinese wine obtainable from the Emporiums.

Beancurd in clay-pot

Recipe: p. 62

15

clockwise — Scrambled Eggs with crabmeat, Fried Beef with Spring Onions, Stuffed Marrow *Recipe: pp. 59, 22, 67*

16

Yuen Tai (top)
Sun Kong Towfoo (bottom)

Recipe: pp. 14, 61

Chinese Beef Steak

Recipe: p. 23

Sweet Sour Pork

Preparation: 30 mins.
Cooking   : 25-30 mins.
Serves   : 4-6

10 ounces (300 g) lean pork
1 teaspoon salt
2 tablespoons sugar
a shake of pepper
1 egg, beaten
4 tablespoons cornflour
1 cucumber
1 onion
2 tomatoes
1 capsicum
1 sprig spring onion
½ tablespoon vinegar
2 tablespoons tomato ketchup
1 teaspoon chilli sauce (optional)
½ teaspoon sesame oil
oil for deep-frying

Clean and cut pork into 1½ inch (3 cm) squares of ½ inch (1 cm) thickness. Season pork with ½ teaspoon salt , ½ teaspoon sugar and pepper . Knead a beaten egg well into the pork. Lastly, mix in 2 tablespoons of cornflour and leave pork to season for at least 30 minutes.
Skin cucumber, quarter it lengthwise, remove the soft centre, and cut each quarter into 1 inch (2 cm) pieces. Cut onion into segments, quarter tomatoes, remove seeds from capsicum and cut into irregular 1 inch (2 cm) pieces. Cut spring onion into 1 inch (2 cm) lengths. Mix together ½ teaspoon salt, sugar, vinegar, tomato ketchup, chilli sauce and sesame oil with ½ cup water for gravy.

Heat oil for deep-frying. Roll seasoned pork pieces in some dry cornflour and fry in hot oil till cooked and crisp. Drain off oil and keep aside.

Remove all but 1 tablespoon oil from the pan. Fry onion segments for one minute before adding the gravy mixture. When gravy boils, add the capsicum, tomatoes and cucumber pieces. Thicken gravy with ½ tablespoon cornflour blended with 2 tablespoons water. Season to taste, then add in the fried pork pieces. Turn off heat at once. Add the spring onion, mix well and serve immediately.

Minced Pork Steamed with Mushrooms

Preparation: 15 mins.
Cooking   : 30 mins.
Serves   : 6-8

6-8 Chinese mushrooms
1 tablespoon soy sauce
2 tablespoons tapioca flour
½ teaspoon salt
shake of pepper
1 pound (450 g) minced pork

Soak mushrooms till soft. Clean them, remove stem and chop finely. Season chopped mushrooms with soy sauce and 1 tablespoon tapioca flour. Mix them well together.

Put minced pork in a bowl, then add 1 tablespoon tapioca flour, salt and a good shake of pepper and knead them well together. While kneading, gradually add 2 tablespoons water. When pork is well kneaded and tacky, knead in mushrooms. Place pork mixture in a heatproof dish and steam over boiling water for 30 minutes.

Note: Instead of mushroom, use either dried squid, preserved cabbage *(tong choy)* or preserved turnip *(tai tow choy)*. This dish can be steamed by placing it on top of the rice just when the rice is drying up. It will be cooked when the rice is cooked.

Mui Choy Chee Yoke
(Pork in Preserved Spinach)

Preparation: 30 mins.
Cooking   2 hrs.
Serves   : 6-8

1 pound (450 g) belly pork
4 tablespoons soy sauce
3 tablespoons oil
4 ounces (100 g) preserved spinach (*mui choy*)
3 shallots, sliced
3 slices ginger
1 tablespoon sugar
1 tablespoon rice wine
1 teaspoon salt

Clean and cut pork into large pieces about 3 inches (7½ cm) wide. It is best to buy a strip 3 inches (7½ cm) wide and cut it into two. Put pork in a pan with enough water to cover and cook for 30 minutes. Remove and drain. Puncture skin all over with a skewer, dab skin dry with a clean cloth and rub 2 tablespoons soy sauce all over skin.

Heat oil for deep-frying. Place pork into hot oil with skin side down and fry for 3-5 minutes until skin is golden brown. To prevent oil from splashing, cover the pan while frying. Remove pork from oil and cool it. When cool enough to handle, cut pork into ½ inch (1 cm) thick pieces. Arrange pieces of pork skin side downwards in a Chinese soup bowl or any heat-proof bowl. Pack slices tightly together.

Soak and wash preserved spinach *(mui choy)*, rinse it in hot water to remove excess salt and squeeze dry. Cut it into 1/10 inch (¼ cm) strips. Heat a clean dry *wok* and fry preserved spinach over medium heat for 5-7 minutes to remove some of the vegetable's strong flavour which may be offensive to some.

Heat 3 tablespoons oil and fry shallots and ginger till lightly browned. Add preserved spinach and toss it in the oil. Add ½ cup water mixed with 2 tablespoons soy sauce, sugar, rice wine and salt. Cover the pan and let it simmer for about 5 minutes.

Spoon the mixture over the pork slices. Put bowl in a steamer and steam for 1 hour over boiling water. Invert bowl on to a warmed serving dish and serve pork hot.

Barbecued Spareribs

Preparation: 5 mins.
Cooking   : 30-40 mins.
Serves   : 4

1¼ pounds (560 g) spareribs
2 tablespoons fish sauce
2 tablespoons *hoi suin* sauce
½ tablespoon black soy sauce
1 tablespoon rice wine
1 tablespoon sugar
few slices of cucumber

Combine the sauces, rice wine and sugar and season the spareribs in this marinade for at least 2 hours, turning them every 30 minutes.

Heat the oven to 450°F (230°C), place the spareribs in a roasting pan and bake for 30 minutes or till meat is cooked and brown. If meat browns too quickly, lower the oven temperature, or switch off after 20 minutes but allow meat to continue cooking in the hot oven. If no oven is available, cook the ribs under a grill or over a charcoal fire, cooking each side for not less than 15 minutes.

Cut ribs apart and serve them garnished with cucumber.

Sweet Sour Spareribs

Preparation : 10 mins
Cooking   : 25 mins.
Serves   : 4

1¼ pounds (560 g) spareribs
3 cloves garlic, chopped fine
1 teaspoon salt
½ tablespoon soy sauce
½ tablespoon rice wine
¼ teaspoon pepper
1 tablespoon tomato ketchup
1 tablespoon Worcestershire sauce
½ teaspoon sesame oil
½ tablespoon sugar
oil for deep-fat frying
3 tablespoons tapioca flour
1 tomato, sliced

Clean and cut spareribs into finger-length pieces. Season ribs with garlic, salt, soy sauce, rice wine and pepper and let it marinate for 1 hour. Mix together tomato ketchup, Worcestershire sauce, sesame oil, sugar and 2 tablespoons water for the gravy.

Heat oil for deep-fat frying. Turn down heat and fry the ribs, coated with tapioca flour, for 5 minutes. Remove from the oil. Reheat oil till smoking hot and re-fry the ribs for another minute. Remove and drain.

Remove all oil from the pan, pour in the well mixed gravy ingredients and let it boil till thick. Add the fried ribs, toss to mix well and serve garnished with tomato slices.

Tow-cheong Chee Yoke
(Shredded Pork with Bean Paste)

Preparation: 15 mins.
Cooking   : 15 mins.
Serves   : 4-6

10 ounces (300 g) pork
1 teaspoon soy sauce
2 teaspoons tapioca flour
1½ teaspoons rice wine
1 sprig spring onion
oil for deep-fat frying
1 tablespoon *tow-cheong (bean paste)*
2 teaspoons sugar

Clean and shred pork thinly and season it with a mixture of soy sauce, tapioca flour and 1 teaspoon rice wine. Leave it in the marinade for 30 minutes. Cut spring onion into 1½ inch (4 cm) lengths.

Heat oil for deep-fat frying and fry pork over a slow fire for 2-3 minutes until pork looks cooked. Remove from oil and drain.

Remove all but 2 tablespoons oil from the pan, heat it and fry bean paste for 2-3 minutes. Add sugar and 2 tablespoons water. When gravy boils, add ½ teaspoon rice wine and fried pork and mix thoroughly. Finally, mix in spring onion, season to taste and serve.

Meat

Shredded Pork with Szechuan Vegetable

Preparation : 25 mins.
Cooking   : 15-20 mins.
Serves   : 4-6

8 ounces (225 g) lean pork
½ teaspoon salt
1 tablespoon tapioca flour
1 teaspoon rice wine
½ teaspoon sesame oil
¼ teaspoon pepper
oil for deep-fat frying
4 shallots, sliced
1 inch (2½ cm) piece of ginger, shredded
½ cup Szechuan vegetable, shredded and
  soaked in water
1 capsicum, shredded
½ cup boiled bamboo shoot, shredded
1 small carrot, boiled and shredded
1 sprig spring onion, cut into 1½ inch (4 cm)
  lengths

Shred pork and marinate it in a mixture of ½ teaspoon salt, ½ tablespoon tapioca flour, 1 teaspoon rice wine and 1 tablespoon water.

For the gravy mix 2 tablespoons water, ½ teaspoon sesame oil, ½ tablespoon tapioca flour and ¼ teaspoon pepper.

Heat oil for deep-fat frying. When oil is hot, fry seasoned pork for 1 minute till it changes colour. Remove and drain well.

Remove all but 1 tablespoon oil from the pan, heat it and brown shallots and ginger. Add Szechuan vegetable and capsicum and fry for 1-2 minutes. Add bamboo shoot, carrot and pork and toss all together. Finally, add gravy mixture and spring onion and toss together for another minute. Season to taste and serve.

Fried Beef with Spring Onion

Preparation: 15-20 mins.
Cooking   : 8 mins.
Serves   : 4-6

10 ounces (300 g) fillet steak
1 teaspoon salt
1 teaspoon soy sauce
shake of pepper
1 tablespoon tapioca flour
¼ teaspoon bicarbonate of soda
3 inch (7½ cm) piece young ginger
5 ounces (150 g) spring onion
1 egg
4 tablespoons oil
1 tablespoon rice wine (optional)

Clean and slice beef very thinly across the grain. Season beef with salt, soy sauce, pepper, tapioca flour and bicarbonate of soda. Knead thoroughly to mix well.

Clean and slice ginger thinly. Rub a little salt into the ginger and wash away the salt after 10 minutes. Clean and cut spring onion into 1½ inch (4 cm) lengths. Beat the egg with a good shake of pepper and ½ tablespoon oil.

Heat the oil and lightly fry ginger for 1 minute. Add beef, spring onion and ½ cup water, and without stirring, cover the pan to cook for 3 minutes. Toss the ingredients together to mix after 3 minutes. Turn off the heat as soon as the ingredients are mixed and the beef has changed colour. Make a well in the centre of the ingredients and pour in the beaten egg. Mix well and serve at once. If desired, add 1 tablespoon rice wine just before serving.

Chinese Beef Steak

Preparation: 10 mins.
Cooking   : 8 mins.
Serves   : 6

1 pound (450 g) fillet steak
¾ teaspoon salt
3½ teaspoons sugar
1 teaspoon bicarbonate of soda
1½ teaspoons soy sauce
2 tablespoons tapioca flour
1 small egg
2 tablespoons Worcestershire sauce
6 tablespoons oil
1 tablespoon tomato ketchup
½ teaspoon sesame oil
¼ teaspoon pepper

Clean fillet steak and cut it into 12-14 pieces, cutting across the grain. Using the back of a chopper, pound the pieces of meat on both sides to tenderize.

Marinate the meat in a mixture of ½ teaspoon salt, ½ teaspoon sugar, bicarbonate of soda, soy sauce, tapioca flour and the egg. Knead meat for at least 5 minutes, adding about 6 tablespoons water gradually. Lastly, add 1 tablespoon Worcestershire sauce and 2 tablespoons oil and knead once again. Leave the meat in the marinade for at least 3 hours.

Mix gravy ingredients: in ¼ cup water, add ¼ teaspoon salt, 3 teaspoons sugar, 1 tablespoon Worcestershire sauce, tomato ketchup, sesame oil and pepper. Mix thoroughly.

Heat 4 tablespoons oil in a frying pan. Fry the steak 6 pieces at a time over high heat. When one side is done, turn over to fry the other side. Each side should not take more than 1 minute. Remove steaks from the pan when they are about half cooked.

In the same pan, cook the gravy mixture, stirring until it boils. Allow the gravy to boil for 2-3 minutes before returning the steaks to the pan. Toss well to mix so that the steaks are evenly coated with gravy. Serve at once.

Braised Beef with Radish

Preparation: 15 mins.
Cooking   : 2½ hrs.
Serves   : 4-6

10 ounces (300 g) shin beef
1 radish
3 tablespoons oil
1 clove garlic, sliced
1 slice ginger
1 segment of star anise
1 onion, quartered
6 peppercorns
4 tablespoons soy sauce
½ tablespoon sugar
½ teaspoon salt

Clean and cut beef into 1½ inch (4 cm) cubes. Cut radish into pieces almost the size of the meat.

Heat 3 tablespoons oil and brown garlic, ginger and onion lightly. Add beef and toss it in oil to seal in the juices. Add 2 cups water, star anise, peppercorns, soy sauce, sugar and salt and simmer in a closed pan for 2 hours.

When beef is tender, add radish and cook for another 30 minutes or until radish is tender. Season to taste and serve garnished with coriander leaves.

Beef in Clay Pot

Preparation: 10 mins.
Cooking   : 1½ hrs.
Serves   : 6-8

6 shallots
1 head of garlic
½ inch (1 cm) piece of ginger
2 sprigs coriander leaves
1¼ pounds (560 g) belly beef
10 peppercorns
1 tablespoon soy sauce
a pinch of mixed spice *(ng heong fun)*
2 tablespoons oil
1 teaspoon sesame oil
2 tablespoons oyster sauce
1 tablespoon black soy sauce
2 teaspoons cornflour
1 tablespoon rice wine

Skin shallots, wash and leave them whole. Separate cloves of garlic, wash them and leave them whole. Slice ginger, chop coriander leaves for garnishing but keep the roots for cooking.

Place beef, coriander roots, peppercorns, soy sauce and mixed spice in a pan with 1 cup water and allow it to simmer slowly. When meat is tender, cut it up into 2 inch (5 cm) square pieces.

Heat the oil with sesame oil in a clay pot and fry shallots, garlic and ginger till they are limp. Add meat stock, oyster sauce and black soy sauce. When it boils, add the meat and cook for another 10 minutes. Thicken the gravy with cornflour blended with 1 tablespoon water. Season to taste and turn off heat. Mix in rice wine and serve garnished with coriander leaves.

Note: If desired, add some Chinese celery *(kun choy)* to the beef for the last 10 minutes of cooking time.

Beef Curry

Preparation: 25 mins.
Cooking   : 1½-2 hrs.
Serves   : 6-8

1¼ pounds (560 g) beef
½ coconut, grated
5 tablespoons oil
3 cloves
2 inch (5 cm) stick cinnamon
2 cardamoms
2 segments of star anise
1 teaspoon cummin
1 inch (2½ cm) piece ginger, shredded
10 shallots, sliced
1 sprig curry leaves or bay leaves
2 tablespoons curry powder
4 green chillies, slit into 4 at the tip
4 potatoes, cubed
1 teaspoon salt
1 lime

Clean and cut beef into 2 inch (5 cm) square pieces of ½ inch (1 cm) thickness. Extract ½ cup first coconut milk and 1½ cups second coconut milk.

Heat the oil and fry cloves, cinnamon, cardamoms, star anise and cummin for 1 minute. Add ginger, shallots and curry leaves and fry for another 2 minutes. Add meat and fry for a few minutes to seal in the juices. Add the second extraction (1½ cups) of coconut milk and cook till meat is tender.

When meat is tender, add curry powder, green chillies and potatoes and cook till curry is thick. Stir frequently to prevent burning. Add the first extraction of coconut milk and salt and cook curry till it is as thick as desired. Squeeze lime juice into the curry and season to taste. Serve with rice or bread.

Note: Fry curry powder in a clean, dry frying pan over low heat for 5 minutes before use.

Beef Kurmah

Preparation: 30 mins.
Cooking   : 1½ hrs.
Serves   : 6-8

1¼ pounds (560 g) beef
2 tablespoons coriander
1 tablespoon cummin
1 dessertspoon aniseed
1 dessertspoon peppercorns
20 almonds
¾ coconut, grated
3 tablespoons ghee *or* oil
16 shallots, sliced
2 cloves garlic, sliced
½ inch (1 cm) piece ginger, shredded
2 inch (5 cm) stick cinnamon
3 cloves
3 cardamoms
1 stick lemon grass
1 teaspoon salt
1 lime

Clean and cut beef into ½ inch (1 cm) thick pieces. Grind or pound together coriander, cummin, aniseed and peppercorns. Grind or pound almonds separately. Extract ½ cup first coconut milk and 1½ cups second coconut milk.

Heat oil or ghee in a pan and fry shallots, garlic and ginger till light brown. Add cinnamon, cloves and cardamoms, bruised lemon grass, coriander, cummin, aniseed and pepper.

Add meat and salt and toss till meat is sealed all over. Stir in the second extraction (1½ cups) of coconut milk, cover the pan and simmer till meat is tender.

When meat is tender, add the first extraction (½ cup) of coconut milk and the ground almonds and continue cooking till gravy is of the right consistency. Add lime juice and season to taste.

Note: The following substitutions may be made: chicken for beef, candlenuts for almonds, milk for coconut milk (though in this case the flavour would not be quite the same). Onions and tomatoes can also be added to the curry with the almonds. This is a white curry, not pungent but very rich.

Beef Rendang

Preparation: 30 mins.
Cooking   : 1½-2 hrs.
Serves   : 6-8

1¼ pounds (560 g) shin beef
15 dried chillies
20 shallots
½ inch (1 cm) piece galingale
5 sticks lemon grass
2 coconuts, grated
5 tablespoons oil
3 pieces *assam gelugur*
1 teaspoon salt
1 turmeric leaf

Clean and cut beef into ½ inch (1 cm) thick pieces. Grind or pound chillies, shallots, galingale and lemon grass. Extract 4 cups of coconut milk from grated coconut.

Heat the oil and fry the ground ingredients for 2-3 minutes. Add meat and fry to seal in the juices. Add coconut milk, bring to the boil and simmer till meat is tender.

When the meat is nearly done, add *assam gelugor* and salt and cook till the curry is almost dry. Add the turmeric leaf. Continue cooking till the curry is dry enough, stirring all the while to prevent burning. Season to taste.

Fried Beef with Oyster Sauce

Preparation : 15 mins.
Cooking   : 12 mins.
Serves   : 4-6

10 ounces (300 g) fillet steak
¼ teaspoon bicarbonate of soda
1 teaspoon salt
1 teaspoon sugar
2 teaspoons soy sauce
1 teaspoon black soy sauce
1 teaspoon sesame oil
1½ tablespoons tapioca flour
¼ teaspoon pepper
oil for deep-fat frying
½ inch (1 cm) piece ginger
1 sprig spring onion
1 small carrot
2 teaspoons oyster sauce
½ tablespoon rice wine

Clean and slice beef very thinly across the grain. Season beef with bicarbonate of soda, ½ teaspoon salt, ½ teaspoon sugar, 1 teaspoon soy sauce, 1 teaspoon black soy sauce, ½ teaspoon sesame oil, 1 tablespoon tapioca flour and a good shake of pepper. Knead beef thoroughly, gradually adding 2 tablespoons water. Lastly, knead in ½ tablespoon oil and allow meat to marinate for 30 minutes.

Clean and slice ginger thinly. Cut spring onion into 1½ inch (4 cm) lengths and carrot into ⅒ inch (¼ cm) slices or fancy shapes.

Mix ingredients for gravy: to 5 tablespoons water, add ½ teaspoon salt, ½ teaspoon sugar, 1 teaspoon soy sauce, 2 teaspoons oyster sauce, ½ teaspoon sesame oil, ½ tablespoon tapioca flour and a good shake of pepper.

Heat 3 cups oil for deep-fat frying. When oil is very hot, put in seasoned beef and remove pan from heat. Fry beef for ½ minute then remove it from the pan. Drain well.

Remove all but 1 tablespoon oil from the pan. Fry the ginger slices and carrot. Add the beef and the well mixed gravy mixture. As soon as it boils, add the spring onion and rice wine. Season to taste and serve.

Spring Rolls

Preparation: 30 mins
Cooking   : 15-20 mins

5 ounces (150 g) pork
6 water chestnuts
½ onion
4 mushrooms
8 ounces (225 g) prawns
¼ teaspoon salt
shake of pepper
2 teaspoons sesame oil
¼ teaspoon mixed spice *(ng heong fun)*
1 egg
2 tablespoons crabmeat (optional)
5 ounces (150 g) mysentery (pig's caul)
6 tablespoons tapioca flour
oil for deep-fat frying
cucumber and tomato slices for garnishing
2 limes.

Filling
Clean and cut pork into ¼ inch (½ cm) strips. Dice water chestnuts, onion and mushrooms. Chop up prawns. Mix pork, water chestnuts, onion, mushrooms prawns and crabmeat, if used, with 1 teaspoon tapioca flour, salt, pepper, sesame oil, mixed spice and egg.

Clean mysentery and cut into 8 inch (20 cm) squares.

Place portions of filling on pieces of mysentery and roll each piece into a neat, tight roll. Coat each roll with tapioca flour and deep-fry in hot oil till golden brown.

Drain well, cut into 1 inch (2½ cm) pieces and serve garnished with cucumber and tomato slices, and lime wedges.

Note: Spring rolls are normally served with spiced salt. To make spiced salt, place 2 tablespoons salt in a clean, dry pan with 1 teaspoon mixed spice and, stirring continuously, fry over low heat for 3 to 4 minutes.

Fried Spring Chicken

Recipe: p 45

Sweet-Sour Spareribs

Recipe: p. 21

Satay

Preparation: 1 ½-2 hours
Cooking   : 10 mins

1 pound (450 g) beef *or* chicken
10 shallots
3 talks lemon grass
1 thin slice galingale
1 inch (2½ cm) piece ginger
½ tablespoon ground coriander
½ teaspoon ground aniseed
1 teaspoon ground cummin
½ cup sugar
1 teaspoon salt
1 teaspoon turmeric powder
½ cup grated coconut
¼ cup oil
Satay sauce
12-15 shallots
2 thin slices galingale
¾ inch (2 cm) piece ginger
1 stalk lemon grass
1 pound (450 g) roasted peanuts
2 tablespoons tamarind
½ cup oil
1 tablespoon ground red chillies
10 tablespoons chopped palm sugar
1 teaspoon salt

Cut the meat into thin bite-sized pieces. Grind shallots, lemon grass, galingale and ginger to a smooth paste. Mix this paste with the ground spices, sugar, salt and turmeric powder. Marinate the meat in this mixture for at least 1 hour before threading on thin satay skewers. The meat can be kept refrigerated overnight in this marinade.

Extract ¼ cup coconut milk from grated coconut. Mix ¼ cup oil with the coconut milk and use this for basting the meat while grilling.

Make a charcoal fire in a charcoal brazier. (Use a rectangular tin with metal grating or wire toaster over the open top if you don't have a proper charcoal brazier.) When ready to start the meal, grill skewered meat over the charcoal fire, basting with the oil and coconut milk mixture till the meat is cooked. If you have a barbecue pit or a few braziers, the guests can join in the fun.

Serve with satay sauce, onion and cucumber wedges, and *lontong* or toast.

Satay sauce
Grind shallots, galingale, ginger and lemon grass. Crush roasted peanuts either with a rolling pin, in a mortar or in a blender. Extract ½ cup tamarind juice from 2 tablespoons tamarind.

Heat ½ cup oil and fry the ground chillies and other ground ingredients till the oil separates from the ingredients. Add crushed peanuts and mix well before adding chopped palm sugar, salt and tamarind juice. Stir the mixture and allow it to simmer till the gravy is thick and oil rises to the top.

This sauce can be kept refrigerated for a few days. Leftover sauce is delicious with rice, potatoes or sliced cucumber.

31

Poultry

Paper-wrapped Chicken

Preparation : 10-15 mins.
Cooking   : 4-5 mins.
Serves   : 6

1½ cups chicken meat
½ inch (1 cm) piece ginger
1 teaspoon soy sauce
2 teaspoons rice wine
¼ teaspoon salt
½ teaspoon sugar
oil for deep-fat frying
12 6-inch (15 cm) square pieces grease-proof
    paper

Cut chicken meat into bite-sized pieces and season with ginger juice, soy sauce, rice wine, salt, sugar and 2 tablespoons oil. Marinate chicken for 30 minutes.

Divide chicken into 12 portions. Place a portion on each piece of well-greased grease-proof paper and wrap firmly to form little packets. Tuck the loose end of the paper into one of the folds or staple it securely.

Heat the oil for deep-fat frying and fry the packets of chicken for 2-3 minutes till paper browns. Drain well and serve.

Chicken Baked in Salt

Preparation : 10-15 mins.
Cooking   : 40-50 mins.
Serves   : 6-8

1 chicken, about 3½ pounds (1½ kg)
1 inch (2½ cm) piece ginger
1 teaspoon salt
pinch of mixed spice *(ng heong fun)*
1 tablespoon rice wine
2 teaspoons soy sauce
2 sheets greaseproof paper
20 pounds (9 kg) rock salt

Clean chicken and cut off legs. Hang it up to dry. Pound ginger and mix it with salt, mixed spice and rice wine. Pour this mixture into the cavity of the chicken and rub the whole interior evenly with it. Leave the chicken to season for 1 hour. Brush skin with soy sauce and wrap chicken in 2 thicknesses of grease-proof paper.

Put rock salt in a large and deep pan and fry it till it is very hot. Make a well in the centre

and embed chicken in the salt. When chicken is completely covered with salt, cover the pan and leave it over low heat for 15 minutes. Turn off the heat and allow the chicken to bake in hot salt for another 15 minutes. It should then be cooked.

Unwrap the chicken very carefully, lift it onto a chopping board and pour out the juice into a bowl. Cut the chicken into bite-sized pieces and arrange them on a serving dish. Pour the juice over the chicken and serve with chilli sauce.

Note: Choose the oldest large pan in your possession, for the rock salt will leave pits behind. Two enamel basins can be used if no large, deep pan is available.

Almond Chicken

Preparation: 30 mins.
Cooking   : 15 mins.
Serves   : 4-6

1 cup almonds
1 leg of chicken, deboned
4 sets of gizzard
3 teaspoons tapioca flour
1 teaspoon soy sauce
2 teaspoons rice wine
½ teaspoon salt
1 cup water chestnuts, diced
oil for deep-fat frying
4 Chinese mushrooms, soaked, cleaned and
   diced
2 onions, diced
¼ teaspoon sugar
½ teaspoon sesame oil
shake of pepper
1 angled loofah, diced
3 teaspoons chopped spring onion
1 sprig coriander leaves

Blanch almonds and dry them. Clean chicken leg and gizzards and dice them into ½ inch (1 cm) cubes. Season chicken meat with 2 teaspoons tapioca flour, ½ teaspoon soy sauce, 1 teaspoon rice wine and ¼ teaspoon salt.

Boil 1 cup water in a pan, add the water chestnuts and bring it back to boil. Remove and drain well. Keep the water for cooking.

Heat 1 cup oil and deep-fry almonds in slightly smoking oil till light brown. Remove then drain. Remove all but 2 tablespoons oil and fry the chicken meat for 1 minute. Then add the gizzards, mushrooms, water chestnuts and onion with ¼ cup water and cook for 3-4 minutes.

Mix ingredients for gravy : to 3 tablespoons water, add 1 teaspoon tapioca flour, ¼ teaspoon salt, ¼ teaspoon sugar, ½ teaspoon soy sauce, ½ teaspoon sesame oil, 1 teaspoon rice wine and a good shake of pepper. Mix well.

When meat is cooked, add the angled loofah, toss to mix well, then add the gravy mixture. When the angled loofah is cooked, season to taste and serve garnished with browned almonds, spring onion and coriander leaves.

Chicken Casserole

Preparation: 20 mins.
Cooking   : 40-50 mins.
Serves   : 4

8 chicken thighs
1 teaspoon salt
shake of pepper
1 onion
1 tin button mushrooms
8 tablespoons oil
4 tablespoons tomato puree
1 tablespoon cornflour
½ teaspoon sugar
1 tablespoon sherry

Clean chicken thighs and season them with salt and pepper. Dice the onion and halve button mushrooms.

Heat the oil and brown each piece of chicken before putting it in the casserole. Remove all but 1 tablespoon oil, lightly brown the diced onion and add tomato puree, cornflour, salt, sugar and pepper well mixed with 1 cup of the mushroom liquid. When gravy boils and thickens, add the mushrooms and sherry. Then pour gravy over the chicken in the casserole.

Cover the casserole and cook it in a moderate oven, 375°F (190°C) for 40 minutes till chicken is tender. Serve casserole with boiled green peas or carrots and buttered rice or riced potatoes.

Note: To make buttered rice, boil rice in the usual way. Mix butter with the hot rice before serving. To make riced potatoes, boil potatoes. When potatoes are cooked, peel them and put them through the potato ricer.

Ayam Golek

Preparation: 40-50 mins.
Cooking   : 1 hr.
Serves   : 6-8

15 dried chillies
5 shallots
2 cloves garlic
½ inch (1 cm) piece ginger
½ inch (1 cm) piece galingale *(lengkuas)*
1½ teaspoons salt
1 stalk lemon grass
1 chicken, about 3½ pounds (1½ kg)
1½ coconuts, grated
2 teaspoons sugar

Grind or pound together chillies, shallots, garlic, ginger, *lengkuas* and salt. Bruise lemon grass by lightly pounding it. Clean chicken and rub a little of the ground ingredients all over it. Put lemon grass into the cavity of the chicken. Place the chicken in a roasting tin and bake in a hot oven, 400°F (200°C).

Add ½ cup water to grated coconut and extract thick coconut milk. Put the rest of the ground ingredients and coconut milk in a saucepan. Add sugar and cook, stirring all the time till the mixture thickens.

After 30 minutes in the oven, baste the chicken with the coconut mixture. Return chicken to the oven. Repeat basting every 5 minutes until chicken is tender and the coconut mixture is used up. Before serving the chicken, pour gravy from the roasting tin all over it.

Steamed Chicken with Sausage

Preparation: 15-20 mins.
Cooking   : 20-30 mins.
Serves   : 4-6

2 cups chicken meat
1½ inch (4 cm) piece ginger
2 tablespoons tapioca flour
2 tablespoons soy sauce
shake of pepper
2 Chinese sausages
4 Chinese mushrooms
2 tablespoons oil
½ teaspoon salt
1 tablespoon rice wine

Cut chicken meat into bite-sized portions. Pound ginger and squeeze for juice. Season chicken with 1 tablespoon tapioca flour, 1 tablespoon soy sauce, ginger juice and pepper.

Slice sausage, wash and quarter mushrooms. Season mushrooms with 1 tablespoon tapioca flour, 1 tablespoon soy sauce, 2 tablespoons oil and ½ teaspoon salt.

Mix chicken meat with sausages and mushrooms and add rice wine and pepper. Place the ingredients in a heat-proof dish and steam over boiling water for 20 minutes. Serve garnished with coriander leaves.

Note: Instead of ginger juice, use ginger slices if desired. This dish can be steamed over rice that is just drying and will be cooked when rice is cooked.

Chicken Legs Stewed with Mushrooms

Preparation : 20 mins.
Cooking   : 40-50 mins.
Serves   : 4

10 chicken legs
1½ tablespoons soy sauce
oil for deep-fat frying
20 Chinese mushrooms
2 teaspoons tapioca flour
6 leaves Chinese cabbage
¾ teaspoon salt
1 teaspoon sugar
1 teaspoon oyster sauce
½ teaspoon sesame oil
shake of pepper
½ inch (1 cm) piece ginger, sliced
2 shallots, sliced
2 cloves garlic, sliced
2 cups chicken stock

Clean chicken legs and season them with 1 tablespoon soy sauce. Heat the oil for deep-fat frying and fry chicken legs in hot oil till they are brown. Cool and cut each into 2 pieces.

Soak and clean mushrooms, remove stems and halve the mushrooms. Season them with tapioca flour, 1 teaspoon soy sauce and 1 tablespoon oil. Clean and cut Chinese cabbage into 2 inch (5 cm) lengths.

Mix gravy ingredients: to 2 cups stock add ½ teaspoon salt, 1 teaspoon sugar, 1 teaspoon soy sauce, 1 teaspoon oyster sauce, ½ teaspoon sesame oil and a good shake of pepper.

Heat 3 tablespoons oil and brown the ginger, shallot and garlic slices. Add mushrooms and chicken legs and stir to mix. Add gravy mixture, cover the pan and allow food to simmer for 30-40 minutes. When cooked, the mushrooms and chicken legs should be tender and the gravy thick. Season to taste.

Boil ½ cup water in another pan. When water boils, add ¼ teaspoon salt and the cabbage leaves. Cover and cook for 2 minutes.

Arrange boiled cabbage leaves on a serving dish and serve mushrooms and chicken legs on the leaves.

Note: For a variation of this dish, try adding sliced tinned abalone to the mushrooms and chicken legs just before serving. Use the abalone liquid as stock for gravy. Abalone should be cooked only long enough to heat it up. Over-cooking toughens it.

Chicken Boiled in Soy Sauce

Preparation: 10 mins.
Cooking   : 40 mins.
Serves   : 6-8

2 tablespoons soy sauce
½ tablespoon black soy sauce
thumb-sized piece rock sugar
1 inch (2½ cm) stick cinnamon
2 segments of star anise
1 chicken, about 3½ pounds (1½ kg) in weight
oil
1 cucumber, sliced
2 tomatoes

In a tall and narrow saucepan, boil 2 cups water with soy sauce, black soy sauce, rock sugar, cinnamon stick and star anise.

Clean chicken and put it into the boiling mixture. Cover the pan and simmer for 15-20 minutes. Turn off the heat and allow chicken to finish cooking for another 20 minutes.

Remove chicken and rub a little oil all over. Cut it into pieces and place on a serving dish, on a bed of sliced cucumber. Garnish with tomato slices. If desired, boil the stock till it is much reduced in quantity, then cool it and pour some over the chicken.

Chicken Curry

Preparation : 40 mins.
Cooking   : 30-40 mins.
Serves   : 6-8

½ coconut, grated
8 cloves garlic
1 inch (2½ cm) piece ginger
1 chicken, about 3½ pounds (1½ kg)
1 tablespoon ground chilli
2 tablespoons curry powder
2 tablespoons margarine
1 sprig curry or bay leaves
8 shallots, sliced
1 lime
1 teaspoon salt

Extract 1 cup first coconut milk and 2 cups second coconut milk. Pound together garlic and ginger. Clean the chicken and cut it into 12-15 pieces. Season the pieces with ground chilli, curry powder, the pounded ginger and garlic, and salt.

Heat the margarine in a pan and fry curry leaves and shallots until shallots are brown. Add seasoned chicken and fry to seal in the juices. Add the second extraction of coconut milk and stir till well mixed. Cover the pan and allow curry to simmer for ½ hour till chicken is tender.

When chicken is tender and curry is fairly thick, add the first extraction of coconut milk and a squeeze of lime juice. Season to taste.

Mild Chicken Curry

Preparation : 40 mins.
Cooking   : 40 mins.
Serves   : 6-8

1 chicken, about 3½ pounds (1½ kg)
15 dried chillies
2 stalks lemon grass
½ inch (1 cm) piece turmeric
1 inch (2½ cm) piece galingale
15 shallots
2 cloves garlic
4 candlenuts
1 × 1 × ¼ inch (2½ × 2½ × ½ cm) piece shrimp paste
1 coconut, grated
5 tablespoons oil
1½ teaspoons salt
10 *daun limau perut,* shredded (optional)

Clean chicken and cut into 12-14 pieces. Pound together chillies, lemon grass, turmeric, galingale, shallots, garlic, candlenuts and shrimp paste. Extract 1 cup first coconut milk and 2 cups second coconut milk.

Heat the oil and fry ground spices till well cooked and fragrant before adding the chicken juices. Add the second extraction of coconut milk, cover the pan and simmer for about 30 minutes till chicken is tender.

When the chicken is tender and curry gravy is thick, add the first cup of coconut milk and shredded *daun limau perut,* if desired, stirring gently for about 3 minutes or till curry is thick and has a thin layer of oil on top. Season to taste and squeeze some lime juice in, if preferred, before serving.

Teochew Duck

Preparation : 15 mins.
Cooking : 100 mins.
Serves : 6-8

1 duck, about 3½ pounds (1½ kg)
1 inch (2½ cm) piece galingale
4 tablespoons oil
3 tablespoons sugar
2 tablespoons soy sauce
1 tablespoon black soy sauce
10 red chillies
3 cloves garlic
4-5 tablespoons vinegar
½ teaspoon salt
sugar to taste

Clean duck and cut off the legs. Slice galingale into 4, stuff the slices into the duck, then dry it.

Heat the oil in a pan and add sugar to it. Stir sugar in the oil till it forms a dark caramel. Put duck into the pan and turn it till it is evenly browned by the caramel. Add soy sauce and black soy sauce and continue turning the duck in it. When the duck is evenly coated, add 3 cups water, cover the pan and allow duck to simmer for 1½ hours till it is tender and gravy is thick. If there is too much gravy, boil quickly for 2-3 minutes to reduce it. Season to taste. Cut into bite-sized pieces and serve.

Note: A strip of belly or shoulder pork can be cooked with duck and served with it. Serve chilli sauce with this dish.

Chillie Sauce

Pound chillies and garlic and mix in vinegar, salt and sugar to get a sauce of the consistency desired.

Duck Stewed with Ginger

Preparation: 40 mins.
Cooking : 25-30 mins.
Serves : 6-8

1 duck, about 3½ pounds (1½ kg)
2 tablespoons soy sauce
2 teaspoons black soy sauce
6 Chinese mushrooms
3 ounces (75 g) young ginger
2 cloves garlic
2 sprig spring onion
10 ounces (300 g) lettuce
½ tablespoon *towcheong*
½ teaspoon salt
1 teaspoon sugar
2 teaspoons sesame oil
shake of pepper
oil for deep-fat frying
1 tablespoon tapioca flour
1 tablespoon rice wine

Clean duck and cut it into about 24 small pieces. Season with 1 tablespoon soy sauce and 1 teaspoon black soy sauce.

Soak mushrooms, remove stems and halve or quarter each, depending on size. Cut the ginger into ¼ inch (½ cm) slices. Chop the garlic. Cut spring onion into 1½ inch (4 cm) lengths and clean lettuce leaves. Pound *towcheong.*

Mix gravy ingredients: to 4 cups water add salt, sugar, sesame oil, pepper, 1 tablespoon soy sauce and 1 teaspoon black soy sauce. Mix well.

Heat the oil for deep-fat frying and fry duck till pieces are brown in colour. Take out browned duck and remove all but 2 tablespoons oil.

In the hot oil, brown garlic and ginger. Then add the *towcheong* and stir-fry for 1 minute. Add the fried duck, mushrooms and gravy mixture. Cover the pan and simmer for at least 1 hour over very low heat. When meat is tender boil quickly to reduce gravy. Thicken gravy by adding tapioca flour blended with 2 tablespoons water. Season to taste. Finally, add rice wine and spring onion. Serve stewed duck on a bed of boiled lettuce.

Chicken Fried with Dried Chillies

Preparation : 20-25 mins.
Cooking   : 5 mins.
Serves   : 4-6

1½ cups chicken meat
½ cup dried chillies
½ inch (1 cm) piece ginger
2 tablespoons soy sauce
3 teaspoons tapioca flour
1 teaspoon Worcestershire sauce
½ teaspoon sesame oil
2 teaspoons rice wine
1 teaspoon sugar
5 tablespoons oil

Cut the chicken meat into bite-sized pieces. Remove stems and seeds from dried red chillies, wash them very quickly, cut them into 1 inch (2½ cm) lengths and dry them in the sun till crisp. Pound ginger and extract ginger juice. Season chicken meat in a marinade of 1 tablespoon soy sauce, 2 teaspoons tapioca flour and ginger juice for at least 30 minutes.

Mix gravy ingredients: to ¼ cup water add 1 teaspoon tapioca flour, 1 tablespoon soy sauce, 1 teaspoon Worcestershire sauce, ½ teaspoon sesame oil, 2 teaspoons rice wine and 1 teaspoon sugar. Mix well together.

Heat the oil and fry dried red chillies over low heat for ½ minute until the chillies are a dark, reddish-brown colour. Add seasoned chicken and fry till chicken pieces are cooked (about 3-4 minutes). Add the gravy mixture and fry till the gravy thickens. Season to taste and serve.

Five Spice Chicken

Preparation : 10-15 mins.
Cooking   : 6-8 mins.
Serves   : 6-8

1 chicken, about 3½ pounds (1½ kg)
1 inch (2½ cm) piece ginger
4 shallots
½ teaspoon mixed spice *(ng heong fun)*
1 teaspoon salt
½ teaspoon sugar
1 tablespoon soy sauce
½ teaspoon sesame oil
1 tablespoon rice wine
¼ teaspoon pepper
1 egg yolk
5 tablespoons cornflour
oil for deep-fat frying

Clean chicken and cut it into 24 pieces. Pound ginger and shallots. Season chicken pieces with pounded ginger and shallots, mixed spice, salt, sugar, soy sauce, sesame oil, rice wine and pepper. Leave it in the marinade for 2 hours. Beat the egg yolk and mix it with the seasoned chicken pieces. Coat each piece in cornflour.

Heat oil for deep-fat frying and fry chicken pieces for about 4-5 minutes till they are golden brown and cooked. Drain well and serve with special salt.

Note: Chicken pieces can be lightly browned hours before they are required, removed from the oil, and fried once more in very hot oil for 1 minute just before serving. This is useful when entertaining, as chicken can then be served crisp and hot.

Fried Prawns with garlic salt

Recipe: p. 58

Fried Mussels in Tow-cheong

Recipe: p. 58

Spring Rolls   *Recipe: p. 26*

41

Yong Towfoo

Recipe: p. 56

Spicy Fried Chicken

Preparation : 10 mins.
Cooking   : 10-15 mins.
Serves   : 6-8

1 chicken, about 3½ pounds (1½ kg) in weight
1½ tablespoons curry powder
1 tablespoon black soy sauce
1 teaspoon salt
¼ teaspoon sugar
10 tablespoons oil
½ inch (1 cm) piece ginger, sliced
2 cloves garlic, sliced
1 sprig curry leaves
2 green chillies, slit into 6 parts
1 onion (optional), sliced

Clean and skin chicken and cut it into 4 pieces. Season with curry powder, black soy sauce, salt and sugar. Leave the chicken to marinade for 1 hour.

Heat the oil and fry ginger, garlic, curry leaves and chillies. Add chicken pieces and fry till well-cooked and brown. If onion is used, add it to the chicken when it is almost done.

Fried Chicken in Oyster Sauce

Preparation : 20 mins.
Cooking   : 30-40 mins.
Serves   : 6-8

1 chicken, about 4½ pounds (2 kg)
1 tablespoon soy sauce
1 teaspoon black soy sauce
6 Chinese mushrooms
1 small carrot
1 stalk spring onion
3 cloves garlic
½ inch (1 cm) piece ginger
1 teaspoon salt
1 teaspoon sugar
1 tablespoon oyster sauce
1 teaspoon sesame oil
½ tablespoon rice wine
shake of pepper
oil for deep-fat frying
1 teaspoon tapioca flour

Clean chicken and cut off the legs. Mix 1 tablespoon soy sauce with ½ teaspoon black soy sauce and rub this mixture all over the chicken, inside and outside.

Clean and cut mushrooms into halves, the carrot into ½ inch (1 cm) slices, and spring onion into 1½ inch (4 cm) lengths. Chop the garlic and pound the ginger to extract juice.

Mix ingredients for gravy: to 3 cups water add 1 teaspoon salt, 1 teaspoon sugar, 1 tablespoon oyster sauce, 1 teaspoon sesame oil, ½ teaspoon black soy sauce, ½ table-spoon rice wine, ginger juice and a good shake of pepper.

Heat the oil for deep-fat frying and fry the chicken (whole) till it is golden brown all over. Remove and drain.

Remove all but 2 tablespoons oil, brown the garlic, then fry mushroom and carrot for 1 minute. Add the gravy mixture and fried chicken, then cover the pan and simmer for about 30 minutes till chicken is tender. If necessary, add more water. Turn chicken every 10 minutes to ensure even cooking.

Remove chicken, mushroom and carrot from the pan. Reduce quantity of the gravy by quick boiling until about 1 cup remains. Blend 1 teaspoon tapioca flour with 1 tablespoon water and thicken the gravy with it. When gravy boils, turn off the heat. Keep the gravy hot till it is required.

Cut the chicken into pieces and arrange neat-ly on a serving plate. Place mushroom, carrot and spring onion on the chicken pieces and pour the gravy over the ingredients before serving.

Fried Chicken Strips with Button Mushrooms

Preparation : 30-40 mins.
Cooking   : 6-10 mins.
Serves   : 6-8

1 chicken, about 3½ pounds (1½ kg)
2 tablespoons tapioca flour
2 teaspoons salt
1 teaspoon sugar
1 egg white, beaten
2 teaspoons sesame oil
oil for deep-fat frying
shake of pepper
2 teaspoons oyster sauce
2 teaspoons soy sauce
½ teaspoon black soy sauce
6 ounces (150 g) mustard green *or* lettuce
1 inch (2½ cm) piece ginger, shredded
2 cloves garlic, chopped
1 cup button mushrooms, sliced
1 tablespoon rice wine

Clean and debone the chicken. Cut chicken meat into strips. Leave aside ½ teaspoon tapioca flour and blend the rest with 1 teaspoon salt, ½ teaspoon sugar, beaten egg white, 1 teaspoon sesame oil, 1 tablespoon oil and a good shake of pepper. Knead this marinade well into the chicken meat and leave for 20 minutes.

Mix gravy ingredients: to ¼ cup water add ½ teaspoon salt, ½ teaspoon sugar, 1 teaspoon sesame oil, 2 tablespoons oyster sauce, 2 teaspoons soy sauce, ½ teaspoon black soy sauce, ½ teaspoon tapioca flour and a good shake of pepper.

Boil 1 cup water in a frying pan. When water boils, add 1 tablespoon oil and ¼ teaspoon salt. Add green vegetable to boiling water and boil to lightly cook the vegetables. Drain vegetable and lay on a serving dish.

Heat the oil for deep-fat frying. When oil is hot, put in the seasoned chicken meat. Stir with chopsticks to separate the strips and cook till chicken changes colour — it takes about 1 minute. Remove chicken meat and drain well.

Remove all but 1 tablespoon oil from the pan. Heat the oil and fry ginger and garlic till they brown. Add the button mushrooms and fried chicken, mix well together, then add the gravy mixture. Stir well till gravy thickens. Now add the rice wine and season to taste. To serve, place chicken strips on the boiled vegetables.

Fried Spring Chicken

Preparation: 25-30 mins.
Cooking   : 5 mins.
Serves   : 6

1 carrot
1 inch (2½ cm) slice green, unripe papaya
3 teaspoons salt
5 teaspoons sugar
2 tablespoons vinegar
3 spring chickens, each about 1 pound (450 g)
1½ inch (4 cm) piece ginger
2 tablespoons soy sauce
1 tablespoon sherry
shake of pepper
oil for deep-fat frying
1 cucumber, sliced
1 tomato, sliced

Slice carrot and green papaya and mix 1 teaspoon salt with it. After 5 minutes wash away the salt and dry sliced vegetable on a paper napkin. Put vegetable in a bowl and mix in 3 teaspoons sugar and the vinegar. Allow vegetable to pickle for at least 3 hours.

Clean spring chickens, cut away legs and hang them up to dry. Pound ginger to extract ginger juice. Mix together ginger juice, soy sauce, sherry, pepper, 2 teaspoons sugar and 2 teaspoons salt. Rub this mixture all over the chickens. Allow chickens to season for at least 2 hours.

Heat the oil for deep-fat frying. When oil is hot, fry each chicken for about 5 minutes till they are golden brown and cooked. Cut chicken in two and serve on a serving dish garnished with cucumber and tomato slices and pickled carrot and papaya. Serve sweet plum sauce *(suin mui cheong)* or chilli sauce with this dish.

Crispy Fried Chicken

Preparation: 20 mins
Cooking   : 20 mins.
Serves   : 6-8

1 chicken, about 3½ pounds (1½ kg)
¾ tablespoon spiced salt
3 inch (7½ cm) stick cinnamon
6 segments of star anise
1 tablespoon honey
1 lime, cut into 4 pieces
oil for deep-fat frying

Clean chicken and chop off the legs. Dry the chicken thoroughly. Rub the inside of the chicken with spiced salt. Put cinnamon and star anise inside chicken and close the opening with a toothpick.

Boil 3 cups water with cinnamon and star anise for 5 minutes. Remove spices from the water. Add honey and lime pieces to the water and let it boil. When water boils, hold the chicken over the boiling water and ladle it over the chicken until the skin tightens and looks shiny.

Hang the chicken in a breezy, sunny spot to dry for 5 hours or until it is completely dry. If it is a wet day, dry chicken in front of a fan.

Heat the oil for deep-fat frying and fry the chicken in hot oil for 8-10 minutes until it is golden brown. Cut chicken into large pieces and serve with spiced salt or chilli sauce and sweet plum sauce *(suin mui cheong)*.

Seafood

Steamed Grouper

Preparation : 25-30 mins.
Cooking   : 12 mins.
Serves   : 4-6

1 grouper, about 1 ⅓ pounds (600 g)
2 ounces (50 g) lean pork
3 Chinese mushrooms
6 thin slices ginger
4 teaspoons chopped spring onion
2 teaspoons chopped coriander leaves
2 tablespoons oil *or* lard
1 teaspoon soy sauce
1 teaspoon sesame oil
a few shakes of pepper

Scale the grouper, remove the entrails and wash. Clean and shred the pork. Soak, clean and cut mushroom into ¹/₁₀ inch (¼ cm) thick slices. Clean and shred the ginger very finely. Clean spring onions and coriander leaves.

In a bowl, mix 4 teaspoons water, 1 table-spoon oil, soy sauce, sesame oil and pepper.

Place the cleaned grouper on an enamel plate, arrange the mushroom and pork neatly on the fish and spoon the gravy mixture over the whole fish. Steam fish over boiling water for 12 minutes.

Remove steamed fish from the steamer, transfer it to a clean and warmed serving plate quickly and pour 1 tablespoon oil which has been well heated over the fish. Garnish fish with spring onion and coriander leaves and serve at once.

Note: White pomfret *(bawah putih* or *bawal tambah)* can be used instead of grouper.

Fried Fish with Turmeric

Preparation : 20 mins.
Cooking   : 10-15 mins.
Serves   : 4-6

1 mackerel *(ikan kembong or tenggiri)*, about
** 1 ⅓ pounds (600 g)**
½ teaspoon salt
2 pieces fresh turmeric
oil for frying

Clean fish. If *ikan tenggiri* is used, cut into ½-inch (1 cm) cutlets. If *ikan kembong* is used, make slits diagonally on either side of the fish.

Pound turmeric till it is very fine. Season cleaned fish with salt and turmeric and leave it for at least 30 minutes.

Fry seasoned fish in hot oil till it is brown on both sides.

Note: For a spicier fried fish, use about 1 tablespoon curry powder instead of turmeric to season the fish.

46

Fish Cakes

Preparation: 30 mins.
Cooking   : 10 mins.
Serves   : 6

10 ounces (300 g) potatoes
10 ounces (300 g) threadfin *(ikan kurau)*
½ onion, diced
oil for deep-fat frying
3-4 teaspoons chopped spring onion
1 large egg
1 teaspoon salt
shake of pepper
1 cup breadcrumbs

Scrub potatoes clean and boil them. Skin boiled potatoes and mash them. Clean fish and steam over boiling water. When cooked, remove skin and bones and flake the flesh. Fry the diced onion in 3 teaspoons hot oil till light brown.

Mix flaked fish, mashed potatoes, browned onion, spring onion, egg yolk, salt and pepper in a bowl. Taste the mixture and add more salt and pepper if necessary.

Flour a pastry board and shape a tablespoonful of the mixture at a time into a round cake.

Beat the egg white in a shallow plate. Spread the breadcrumbs on a sheet of greaseproof paper or plastic. Coat the fish cakes with egg white and then toss in the breadcrumbs.

Deep-fry fish cakes till golden brown, drain well and serve.

Egg and Fish Roll

Preparation: 45-50 mins.
Cooking   : 30 mins.
Serves   : 6

1⅓ pounds (600 g) Spanish mackerel *(ikan tenggiri)*
2 teaspoons tapioca flour
1½ teaspoons salt
shake of pepper
3 eggs
¼ tablespoon oil

Clean fish and fillet it. With a tablespoon, scrape off all the flesh from bones and skin. Pound the flesh in a mortar until it becomes a smooth paste.

Return the paste to a big bowl and add tapioca flour, 1 teaspoon salt, a good shake of pepper and about 5 tablespoons water. Stir ingredients together quickly to get a well blended tacky paste. If paste looks firm and

thick, add more water to it. The paste should be soft and sticky.

Beat the eggs with ½ teaspoon salt. Heat ¼ tablespoon oil in a frying pan and make 3 thin omelettes.

Spread the omelettes on a chopping board and spread a portion of fish paste on each omelette. Use a wet knife to prevent paste sticking to it. The paste should be evenly spread over the whole surface of the omelette. Roll up each omelette into a tight roll. Place the rolls in a steamer and steam over boiling water for 30 minutes.

Slice the egg and fish roll into ¼ inch (½ cm) slices and serve with chilli sauce.

Sweet Sour Fish

Preparation: 30 mins.
Cooking   : 10-15 mins.
Serves   : 4-6

1 pomfret *(ikan bawal)*, **about 1⅓ pounds**
   (600 g)
1½ teaspoons salt
2½ teaspoons sugar
1 egg white
6 tablespoons cornflour
4 tablespoons tomato sauce
½ tablespoon vinegar
5 stalks spring onions
5 stalks coriander leaves
2 cloves garlic
oil for deep-fat frying
½ cucumber
1 chilli

Scale the pomfret and remove entrails. Remove the head and slit it in half, taking care not to cut through the skin at the top of the head. Fillet the fish. Score the 2 pieces of fish lengthwise and crosswise without cutting through the skin.

In a big, flat plate, mix 1 teaspoon salt, ½ teaspoon sugar, 1 egg white, 3 tablespoons cornflour and 3 tablespoons water. Marinate the fillets and the fish head too, if preferred, in this mixture. Leave the fish in the marinade for 15-20 minutes.

Clean and shred cucumber, chilli and spring onions. Cut the coriander leaves into 1 inch (2½ cm) lengths and chop the garlic finely. In a bowl, mix ½ cup water, the tomato sauce and vinegar, 2 teaspoons sugar and ½ teaspoon salt together with 2 teaspoons cornflour.

Heat enough oil for deep-fat frying. Dredge seasoned fish with cornflour and fry in hot oil till brown and crisp. Place fried fish on a warmed serving dish.

In a clean frying pan, heat 2 teaspoons oil and brown the garlic. Add the tomato sauce mixture, stirring gently till gravy boils and thickens. Season this gravy well before pouring over the fried fish. Garnish fish with shredded cucumber around it, and chillies, spring onion and coriander leaves on top of it.

Sambal Ikan Bilis

Preparation: 20-25 mins.
Cooking   : 10 mins.
Serves   : 4

8 dried chillies
8 shallots
3 candlenuts
1 × 1 × 1 inch (2½ × 2½ × 2½ cm) piece
   shrimp paste
1 tablespoon tamarind
¼ cup oil
¾ cup ikan bilis
½ teaspoon salt
1 teaspoon sugar

Pound together chillies, shallots, candlenuts and shrimp paste till fine. Squeeze tamarind in ½ cup water to get tamarind juice. Remove head and entrails from ikan bilis, wash them quickly and drain to dry.

Heat ¼ cup oil and fry ikan bilis till crisp and brown. Take them out and leave aside.

Fry pounded ingredients in the same oil for 2-3 minutes. Add tamarind juice, salt and sugar and cook it slowly till gravy it thick. Season to taste, add fried ikan bilis and remove from fire at once.

Note: A sliced onion may be added if desired. Fry the onion with the pounded ingredients.

Otak-Otak

Preparation: 40-50 mins.
Cooking   : 20 mins.
Serves   : 4

10 ounces (300 g) threadfin *(ikan kurau)*
6 dried red chillies
6 shallots
12 peppercorns, optional
1 stalk lemon grass
1 slice galingale
1 × 1 × ¼ inch (2½ × 2½ × ½ cm) piece
** shrimp paste**
2 candlenuts
1 clove garlic
½ inch piece turmeric
5 *daun limau perut*
½ coconut, grated
2 eggs
½ teaspoon sugar
½ teaspoon salt
6-8 pieces banana leaves, 6-8 inches (15-20 cm)
** square**
6-8 leaves of *daun kadeok*
6-8 coconut leaf veins of 1 inch (2½ cm) length,
** or a stapler**

Slice fish into ½ inch (1 cm) slices. Pound together very finely dried chillies, shallots, peppercorns, lemon grass, lengkuas, shrimp paste, candlenuts, garlic and turmeric. Shred *daun limau perut* very finely. Add a little water to the grated coconut and extract ½ cup coconut milk. Beat the eggs with a wooden spoon in a big bowl and add the pounded ingredients, sugar, salt, *daun limau perut* and coconut milk. Mix well.

Scald banana leaves to soften them. Wash and dry the leaves. On each piece of banana leaf, place one piece of *daun kadeok,* 2 slices of fish and over this put 3-4 dessertspoons of the egg mixture. Wrap neatly and fasten with coconut leaf veins or a stapler. Continue wrapping until all the ingredients are used up.

Steam the packets over boiling water for 15-20 minutes.

Note: Fish roe, fish ball paste, mackerel *(ikan tenggiri)* or sole *(ikan lidah)* can be used instead of threadfin. Instead of individual packets, otak-otak can be cooked in a heat-proof dish. In this case, steam over slowly boiling water for about 1 hour to get a smooth custard.

Fish Masak Lemak

Preparation: 30 mins.
Cooking   : 20 mins.
Serves   : 4

8 dried chillies
5 shallots
1 inch (2½ cm) piece ginger
1 x 1 x ¼ inch (2½ x 2½ x ½ cm) piece shrimp
** paste**
1 teaspoon salt
½ coconut, grated
1 stalk lemon grass
5 *daun limau perut* **(optional)**
1 white pomfret *(ikan bawal putih),* **about 1**
** pound (450 g)**

Pound together chillies, shallots, ginger, shrimp paste and salt. Bruise lemon grass and finely shred *daun limau perut*. Extract ½ cup thick coconut milk. Then add 1 cup water to grated coconut and extract a full cup of milk.

Put the second extraction of coconut milk, pounded ingredients and bruised lemon grass into a pan and let it boil slowly till it is fairly thick. While gravy is boiling, scale the fish and remove entrails. Clean it and cut it into 4 or 5 pieces. Rub each piece very lightly with salt.

When gravy is thick enough, put fish into it and let it simmer till fish is cooked. Add the first extraction of coconut milk and shredded *daun limau perut* and continue cooking till oil rises to the top. Season well before serving.

Note: Threadfin *(ikan senangin)* can be used instead of white pomfret.

Acar Fish — Pickled Fish

Preparation: 20 mins.
Cooking   : 15 mins.
Serves   : 4-6

1 Spanish mackerel *(ikan tenggiri),* about 1⅓
  pounds (600 g)
1 teaspoon salt
8 shallots
8 cloves garlic
3 inch piece turmeric
2 chillies
4 tablespoons oil
½ cup vinegar
4 teaspoons sugar

Cut fish into ½ inch (1 cm) cutlets. Wash them and drain, then rub a little salt into each cutlet. Skin shallots, garlic and turmeric. Slice them thinly and dry the slices in the sun for 2-3 hours. Remove seeds from chillies and shred very thinly. Dry well.

Heat 4 tablespoons oil and fry fish cutlets till evenly browned on both sides. Lay them as flat as possible in an enamel bowl or earthenware jar.

Remove all but 1 tablespoon oil from the frying pan and fry dry turmeric in oil till oil is yellow in colour. Remove turmeric and add vinegar, salt and sugar. When vinegar comes to a boil, lower heat and taste it. Add more salt and sugar, if necessary.

Sprinkle shredded chillies and the dry shallot and garlic slices over the fish cutlets and pour vinegar mixture over it. Let fish soak in vinegar for at least 6 hours before serving. It is best to make it the day before serving.

Note: Pickled fish will keep very well in the refrigerator for a week.

Fried Stuffed Hardtail

Preparation : 20 mins.
Cooking   : 20 mins.
Serves   : 4

2 red chillies
3 shallots
1 tablespoon dried prawns
1 medium-sized hardtail *(ikan cencaru)*
1 teaspoon salt
oil for frying
¼ teaspoon sugar
1 lime

Pound together chillies and shallots till fine. Wash dried prawns and pound them separately. Clean the fish which has been skinned and make a slit on each side along the back fin. Rub salt all over the fish.

Heat 2 tablespoons oil and fry pounded chillies and shallots 2-3 minutes before adding dried prawns and sugar. Fry all together till well mixed.

Wash the fish once more to remove excess salt and dry it. Stuff slits and the cavity of the fish with the fried ingredients.

Heat 4 tablespoons oil and fry the fish in it till it is well cooked and brown on both sides. This takes about 5 minutes for each side. Serve fish with lime wedges.

Steamed Melon Soup

Recipe: p. 80

Loh Hon Chye (top)
Chicken Casserole (bottom)

Recipes: pp. 67, 33

Gulai Assam Pedas

Preparation : 25 mins.
Cooking   : 20 mins.
Serves   : 4-6

1⅓ pounds (600 g) piece wolf herring *(ikan parang)*
1 teaspoon salt
8 red chillies
15 shallots
1 inch (2½ cm) piece fresh turmeric
2 stalks lemon grass
1 × 1 × ¼ inch (2½ × 2½ × ½ cm) piece shrimp paste
2 pieces *assam gelugur*

Clean the fish and rub a little salt all over it. Pound together chillies, shallots, turmeric, lemon grass and shrimp paste.

Stir the pounded ingredients and the *assam gelugur* in 1 cup water in a pan and let it simmer for 5-10 minutes to blend the flavours of the pounded ingredients and the *assam gelugur.*

Add the fish and ½ teaspoon salt and let it simmer for another 10 minutes or till fish is cooked. Season to taste by adding more salt, if necessary. A good pinch of sugar may be added, if preferred.

Note: Long beans cut into 1½ inch (4 cm) lengths can be added to this curry if desired.

Gulai Tumis

Preparation : 25 mins.
Cooking   : 15 mins.
Serves   : 4-6

1 white pomfret *(ikan bawal putih)*, about 1⅓ pounds (600 g)
2 stalks lemon grass
12-15 shallots
6 cloves garlic
8-10 red chillies
1 inch (2½ cm) piece fresh turmeric
1 × 1 × ¼ inch (2½ × 2½ × ½ cm) piece shrimp paste
1 tablespoon tamarind

Clean the fish and cut it into 5 or 6 pieces. Clean and slice lemon grass. Pound it together with shallots, garlic, chillies, turmeric and shrimp paste. Prepare 1 cup tamarind juice from the tamarind and strain it.

Heat 4-5 tablespoons oil in an earthenware pot *(belanga)* and fry pounded ingredients for 2-3 minutes till the oil separates from the ingredients.

Add salt and tamarind juice and let it come to a boil before adding the fish. Allow fish to simmer slowly for 10 minutes till cooked. Season to taste.

Note: Other fish that can be used are black pomfret *(ikan bawal hitam)* and threadfin *(ikan kurau).*

Yong Towfoo
(Stuffed Beancurd)

Preparation: 1 hour
Cooking   : 20 mins.
Serves   : 4-6

10 ounces (300 g) Spanish mackerel *(ikan*
   tenggiri)
10 firm white bean curd
4 red chillies
1½ teaspoons salt
1 teaspoon tapioca flour
½ teaspoon sugar
1 teaspoon soy sauce
shake of pepper
4 tablespoons oil
4 spring onions, cut into 1 inch (2½ cm) lengths

Clean the fish and make fish paste (refer to the 'Egg and Fish Roll' recipe).

Wash bean curd and cut each piece diagonally into 2 triangular pieces. Make a deep slit along the diagonal edge, leaving the other 2 edges intact. Slit chillies lengthwise and remove seeds. Stuff bean curd and chillies with fish paste, using a knife which is dipped into salt water frequently to prevent sticking and to give a smooth finish.

Prepare the gravy: mix ½ teaspoon tapioca flour, ½ teaspoon salt, ½ teaspoon sugar, 1 teaspoon soy sauce and a good shake of pepper with ¼ cup water.

Heat 4 tablespoons oil and fry bean curd and chillies lightly with fish side in the oil. When the fish side is lightly brown, add ½ cup water and cook gently for 15 minutes.

Mix the gravy well and add it to the bean curd together with the spring onions. Season well before serving. If preferred, add 1 teaspoon sesame oil. Serve with chilli sauce.

Note: Other vegetables like eggplant, okra and bitter gourd can also be stuffed and served in this dish.

Sambal Prawns

Preparation: 30 mins.
Cooking   : 15 mins.
Serves   : 4-6

10 ounces (300 g) medium-sized prawns
½ teaspoon sugar
1 teaspoon salt
12 red chillies
12 shallots
1 stalk lemon grass
3 candlenuts
1 × 1 × ¼ inch (2½ × 2½ × ½ cm) piece
   shrimp paste
1 tablespoon tamarind
4 tablespoons oil
4 tomatoes, quartered

Shell and devein the prawns. Season with sugar and ½ teaspoon salt. Pound together chillies, shallots, lemon grass, candlenuts and shrimp paste. Prepare ½ cup tamarind juice from 1 tablespoon tamarind. Strain it.

Heat 4 tablespoons oil and fry pounded ingredients till well cooked (about 3-4 minutes). Add prawns and continue stirring till prawns are lightly cooked. Add tomatoes and tamarind juice and simmer till prawns are cooked, tomatoes are tender and gravy is beginning to thicken. Season according to taste before serving.

Prawns And Pineapple Curry

Preparation: 30 mins.
Cooking   : 25-30 mins.
Serves   : 4-6

½ pineapple
10 ounces (300 g) medium-sized prawns
1½ teaspoons salt
½ coconut, grated
10 red chillies
10 shallots
5 candlenuts
1 stalk lemon grass
1 inch (2½ cm) galingale
1 inch (2½ cm) turmeric
1 x 1 x ¼ inch (2½ x 2½ x ½ cm) piece shrimp
  paste
5 tablespoons oil

Skin, quarter and cut off the hard central core of the pineapple. Slice each quarter into ½ inch wedge-shaped pieces. Shell, devein and season prawns with a little salt. Extract ½ cup first coconut milk and 1 cup second coconut milk. Grind together chillies, shallots, candlenuts, lemon grass, galingale, turmeric and shrimp paste.

Heat the oil in a clay pot and fry the ground ingredients till the oil separates from the ingredients. Add the prawns and cook for another 2 minutes.

Add half of the second extraction of coconut milk to help cook the prawns thoroughly. Take out the prawns and set them aside. Add the rest of the second extraction of coconut milk and when it boils again, add the pineapple wedges and 1 teaspoon salt. Let it simmer slowly till pineapple is tender (about 15 minutes).

Return prawns to the curry and add the first extraction of coconut milk, stirring all the while until the curry boils again. Turn off heat immediately and season the curry before serving.

Fried Tamarind Prawns

Preparation: 25 mins.
Cooking   : 15-20 mins.
Serves   : 6-8

1⅓ pounds (600 g) large prawns
2 tablespoons tamarind
1½ teaspoons salt
½ teaspoon sugar
5 tablespoons oil
½ cucumber, sliced

Cut away the whiskers and the sac from the head of the prawns and remove shell between the head and tail. Slit the back of the shelled portion and devein.

Mix tamarind with salt, sugar and 2 tablespoons water. Marinate prawns in this mixture for at least 1 hour.

Heat 5 tablespoons oil and fry the prawns till they are dark brown on both sides. Serve garnished with cucumber slices.

Note: Bawal hitam or *ikan tenggiri* can be used instead of prawns.

Fried Prawns with Garlic Salt

Preparation: 20 mins.
Cooking   : 4-5 mins.
Serves   : 6-8

1⅓ pounds (600 g) medium-sized prawns
1 teaspoon salt
6 cups oil
2 shallots, sliced
6 cloves garlic, chopped finely
½ red chilli, chopped finely
2 tablespoons sherry *or* rice wine
shake of pepper

Leave the prawns unshelled but cut away whiskers and legs and remove the sac from the head. Wash in salt water to remove any sliminess from the shell, then drain and dry.

Heat 6 cups oil for deep-fat frying. When oil is smoking hot, fry the prawns till they are cooked. This takes about 2 minutes. Remove prawns from oil and keep aside.

Pour out all the oil from the pan. In the same pan, coated with oil, fry shallots and garlic till light brown. Then add the chilli, salt and sherry, and finally the fried prawns. Toss all together and remove at once. Dust with a little pepper and serve immediately.

Note: A pinch of mixed spice *(ng heong fun)* can be added to this dish, if desired.

Mussels in Tow-cheong

Preparation: 20 mins.
Cooking   : 10 mins.
Serves   : 4-6

1⅓ pounds (600 g) mussels
3 cloves garlic
3 shallots
1 inch (2½ cm) piece ginger
1 red chilli
1 tablespoon *tow-cheong*
3 tablespoons oil
1 teaspoon sugar

Put mussels in a colander and agitate colander under a running tap to get rid of all the sand. Take each mussel and try to slide the 2 halves of the shell across each other. If they slide, they will be filled with mud and should be discarded. Leave fresh mussels in a basin of water for at least 1 hour.

Chop the garlic and shallots. Shred ginger finely and cut chillies into 1/12 inch (1/5 cm) rings. Chop or pound *tow-cheong* till it becomes a paste.

Heat the oil in a *wok* and lightly brown garlic and shallots. Add *tow-cheong* paste and stir gently for 3-4 minutes. Add ginger, chillies and mussels and stir-fry over high flame for a minute before adding sugar. Continue stir-frying till mussels are all split, indicating that they are cooked. If necessary, reduce gravy a little. Season and serve immediately.

Eggs and Soybean

Scrambled Eggs with Crabmeat

Preparation: 10-15 mins.
Cooking   : 5-8 mins.
Serves   : 4-6

¼ cup bamboo shoots
1 onion
1 stalk spring onion
5 eggs
1½ teaspoons salt
1 teaspoon sesame oil
shake of pepper
6 tablespoons oil
½ cup crabmeat

Shred bamboo shoot and onion. Squeeze out water from the bamboo shoot. Cut spring onion into 1½ inch (4 cm) lengths.

Beat the eggs with salt, sesame oil, pepper and 1 tablespoon oil. Mix in the well-cleaned crabmeat, bamboo shoot and spring onion.

Heat 5 tablespoons oil in a pan and fry onion till limp. Add the egg mixture and scramble till it just begins to set and is lightly cooked. Serve at once with a good shake of pepper.

Note: For variety, scramble eggs with prawns and angled loofah, Chinese sausages and onions, and steamed pig's brain.

Kwai Fah Chee (Shark's Fin with Eggs)

Preparation: 4 hours
Cooking   : 10 mins.
Serves   : 4-6

1 cup shark's fin
4 cups chicken stock
¼ cup water chestnuts
1 stalk spring onion
4 eggs
1 cup crab meat
1 teaspoon salt
1 teaspoon monosodium glutamate
a pinch of ground cinnamon·
shake of pepper
5½ tablespoons lard

Soak shark's fin in hot water till it is soft and loose. Drain, then boil in chicken stock for about 4 hours. Rinse in cold water, drain and remove bits of skin which may be found stuck to the shark's fin.

Peel and shred water chestnuts and cut spring onion into 1½ inch (4 cm) lengths. Heat 1 cup water in a pan and when it boils, add water chestnuts. As soon as water re-boils, turn off the heat and drain water chestnuts.

Beat the eggs and add shark's fin, crab meat, water chestnuts and spring onion. Also add salt, monosodium glutamate, cinnamon and pepper with 1 tablespoon lard.
Mix the ingredients well.

Heat 4 tablespoons lard in a pan. When it is hot, pour in the mixed ingredients and scramble till it sets very lightly. Just when the mixture begins to set, add ½ tablespoon lard and continue to scramble till it is completely set. Serve immediately with a good shake of pepper.

Note: If water chestnuts are not available, use bamboo shoot instead. Kwai Fah Chee is often served with lettuce leaves.

Bean Curd with Vegetables

Preparation: 20 mins.
Cooking   : 6-7 mins.
Serves   : 4

3 × 6 inch (7½ × 15 cm) piece soft bean curd
8 ounces (225 g) lean pork
1 medium-sized carrot
6 cobs young corn
6 water chestnuts
2 shallots
2 cloves garlic
1 cup snow peas
2 teaspoons soy sauce
1 teaspoon oyster sauce
½ teaspoon sesame oil
1 teaspoon salt
½ teaspoon sugar
shake of pepper
5 tablespoons oil
1 tablespoon rice wine
1 teaspoon tapioca flour

Wash the bean curd, place it in an ice tray and freeze it for at least 12 hours. Defrost it before it is required and press out the water. With the knife held at an angle of 45°, slice the bean curd into ¼ inch (½ cm) slices.

Clean and slice the pork, carrot, corn shoots and water chestnuts. Chop shallots and garlic. String the snow peas. Mix gravy ingredients: in ½ cup water mix soy sauce, oyster sauce, sesame oil, salt, sugar and pepper.

Heat 2 tablespoons oil and fry snow peas till they are lightly cooked. Take out and keep aside.

Heat 3 tablespoons oil, brown shallots and garlic and fry pork slices till the pieces separate. Add the bean curd, carrots, corn shoots and water chestnuts and fry all together till well mixed. Add the gravy mixture, cover the pan and cook for 3-4 minutes. When vegetables are cooked, add the snow peas and tapioca flour blended with 1 teaspoon water. Add the rice wine before seasoning to taste. Sprinkle with pepper before serving.

Note: Bean curd prepared this way has a very different texture that somewhat resembles tripe. Instead of pork, prawns may be used.

Mah Poh Towfoo
(Bean Curd in Chilli Sauce)

Preparation : 15 mins.
Cooking   : 10 mins.
Serves   : 4-6

4 soft bean curd squares
2 shallots
2 cloves garlic
½ inch (1 cm) piece ginger
2 stalks spring onions
1 tablespoon *tow-cheong*
½ teaspoon monosodium glutamate
2 teaspoons soy sauce
shake of pepper
5 tablespoons oil
1 cup minced pork
2 teaspoons ground chilli
1 tablespoon rice wine
1 teaspoon tapioca flour

Cut bean curd into 1 inch (2½ cm) cubes. Chop shallots, garlic and ginger. Dice spring onions and chop *tow-cheong* to a paste. Mix gravy ingredients: to ½ cup water add monosodium glutamate, soy sauce and pepper.

Heat 4 tablespoons oil and fry shallots, garlic and ginger for 1 minute. When they begin to brown, add the *tow-cheong* paste and ground chilli. Fry for another minute before adding the pork. Stir well to separate pork and fry till it is cooked.

Add bean curd cubes to the meat mixture, then the rice wine. Mix carefully so as not to break the bean curd before adding the gravy mixture. Cook slowly for about 5 minutes. Slow cooking is necessary to keep bean curd tender. Thicken gravy with tapioca flour blended with 1 tablespoon water. Season to taste. Add spring onion and 1 tablespoon oil before serving.

Note: The amount of ground chilli used depends on individual taste.

Sun Kong Towfoo
(Bean Curd with Crabmeat)

Preparation: 20 mins.
Cooking   : 15-20 mins.
Serves   : 4-6

6 × 4 × 2 inch (15 × 10 × 5 cm) piece soft bean
curd
¼ cup lean pork
1 small carrot
½ cup button mushrooms
2 stalks spring onions
15 snow peas
1 teaspoon salt
½ teaspoon monosodium glutamate
2 teaspoons fish sauce
½ teaspoon sugar
1 teaspoon oyster sauce
½ teaspoon sesame oil
shake of pepper
oil for deep-fat frying
3 slices ginger
¼ cup crabmeat
1 teaspoon tapioca flour
1 egg

Wash the bean curd carefully and chill it for at least 4 hours. Cut it into half lengthwise, then cut each half into 6 equal slices just before cooking. Slice pork, carrot and button mushrooms. Cut spring onions into 1½ inch (4 cm) lengths. String and wash the snow peas.

Mix gravy ingredients: to 1 cup water add salt, monosodium glutamate, fish sauce, sugar, oyster sauce, sesame oil and pepper. Mix well.

Heat the oil for deep-fat frying and fry cold bean curd till brown on both sides. Remove the bean curd to a dish.

Remove all but 2 tablespoons oil from the pan. Fry snow peas with a pinch of salt till they turn bright green. Take them out and leave them with the bean curd.

Heat another 2 tablespoons oil and fry ginger slices till they begin to brown. Add the pork, carrots and button mushrooms and toss together for another minute or two. Then add the gravy mixture and allow it to boil for 1 minute before adding the fried bean curd and snow peas. After another 2 or 3 minutes, add the crabmeat. Blend tapioca flour with 1 tablespoon water and thicken gravy with it. Season to taste and turn off heat.

Add spring onion, an egg which has been beaten, and 1 tablespoon oil to the hot food, stir well and serve with a good shake of pepper.

Note: Use the type of bean curd that is made in a slab. The side edges are firmer and easier to handle than the centre which is much softer and difficult to fry without breaking up. Celery may be used instead of snow peas if the latter is not available.

Bean Curd in Clay Pot

Preparation : 20 mins.
Cooking   : 20-25 mins.
Serves   : 4-6

4 pieces soft bean curd squares
5 ounces (125 g) pork
½ cup bamboo shoot
1 small carrot
½ inch (1 cm) piece ginger
5 Chinese mushrooms
2 red chillies
6 stalks mustard green *(choy sum)*
2 cloves garlic
2 teaspoons soy sauce
½ teaspoon black soy sauce
2 teaspoons oyster sauce
1 teaspoon sesame oil
½ teaspoon salt
2 teaspoons sugar
shake of pepper
oil for deep-fat frying
1 tablespoon *tow-cheong*
½ teaspoon tapioca flour

Wash and cut bean curd diagonally across into 8 triangular pieces. Slice pork, bamboo shoot, carrot and ginger. Soak the mushrooms. When they soften, clean and halve them. Remove seeds from chillies and cut each diagonally into 6-8 pieces. Clean and pluck mustard greens into 2 inch (5 cm) lengths. Chop the garlic.

Mix gravy ingredients: to 1 cup water add

the soy sauce, black soy sauce, oyster sauce, sesame oil, salt, sugar and pepper.

Heat the oil for deep-fat frying and fry bean curd pieces till they are brown. Drain well and keep aside.

In a clay pot heat 4 tablespoons oil and brown ginger slices and garlic. Add the *tow-cheong* and fry for 2 minutes. Then add pork, bamboo shoot, mushroom, carrot and chilli and fry together for another 2 minutes. Add the fried bean curd and gravy mixture. Cover the pot and let the contents simmer for 10 minutes.

Boil 1 cup water with 1 tablespoon oil in a pan. When water boils, put in mustard greens, cover and cook for 2 minutes till greens are cooked. Drain well.

Thicken gravy in the clay pot by adding the tapioca flour blended with 2 teaspoons water. Season to taste and arrange mustard greens all round the top. Sprinkle with a good shake of pepper and serve.

Sambal Telur

Preparation: 30 mins.
Cooking   : 5-10 mins.
Serves   : 5

5 eggs
12 red chillies
10 shallots
1 × 1 × ¼ inch (2½ × 2½ × ½ cm) piece shrimp paste
1 stalk lemon grass
½ coconut, grated
1 tablespoon tamarind
1 teaspoon salt
4 tablespoons oil

Hard-boil the eggs, shell and halve them. Arrange the egg halves on a serving dish, yolk side up.

Grind together chillies, shallots, shrimp paste and lemon grass. Extract 1 cup milk from the grated coconut. Add 3 tablespoons water to the tamarind and extract juice.

Heat 4 tablespoons oil in a pan and fry ground ingredients and salt for about 3 minutes. Add the coconut milk and allow sambal to cook for 2-3 minutes before adding the tamarind juice. Season to taste and pour this sambal over the boiled eggs. Serve with cucumber slices and rice.

Paper-wrapped chicken

Recipe: p. 32

Chicken Rice in Clay-pot (Top)
Kerabu Timun (Bottom)

Recipes: pp. 10, 74

64

Gado Gado

Recipe: p. 70

Mee Siam

Recipe: p. 97

Vegetables

Stuffed Marrow

Preparation : 30-35 mins.
Cooking   : 40 mins.
Serves   : 4-6

1 vegetable marrow
¼ cup shrimps
½ onion
¼ cup minced pork
1 tablespoon diced yam bean *(bangkwang)*
1½ teaspoons tapioca flour
½ teaspoon salt
½ teaspoon sesame oil
shake of pepper
6 tablespoons oil
2 teaspoons chopped spring onion

Scrape off the skin of the vegetable marrow, clean it and scoop out the central pith with a teaspoon. Shell, clean and chop the shrimps. Dice the onion to get 1 tablespoon diced onion. Mix chopped shrimps, minced pork, yam beam, onion, 1 teaspoon tapioca flour,

½ teaspoon salt, 1 teaspoon sesame oil and a good shake of pepper. Knead the mixture to get the ingredients well-mixed and tacky. Stuff the vegetable marrow with this mixture.

Heat the oil in a saucepan large enough to hold the marrow and fry the marrow, turning it frequently till evenly browned. Add 1 cup water with ¼ teaspoon salt to the pan. Cover the pan and allow the vegetable marrow to simmer for 30 minutes till it is tender.

Blend ½ teaspoon tapioca flour with 1 table-spoon water and thicken the gravy with this mixture. Add the spring onion, season to taste and serve whole or sliced.

Loh Hon Chye (Mixed Vegetables)

Preparation : 15 mins.
Cooking   : 15-20 mins.
Serves   : 4-6

1 head mustard greens *(kai choy)*
1 carrot
6 Chinese mushrooms
6 tablespoons oil
2 shallots, sliced
1 teaspoon salt
½ teaspoon monosodium glutamate
½ cup button mushrooms
¼ cup straw mushrooms
12 fried gluten balls *(min kun)*
½ teaspoon tapioca flour

Clean and cut mustard greens into 1 inch (2½ cm) lengths and slice the carrot. Soak the mushrooms to soften, then cut into halves.

Heat 5 tablespoons oil, brown sliced shallots

and fry mustard greens for 1 minute. Add carrot and Chinese mushrooms and toss all together till well mixed. Add salt and mono-sodium glutamate mixed in ½ cup water. Cover the pan and allow vegetables to simmer for 10 minutes.

When vegetables are tender, add button mushrooms, straw mushrooms and fried gluten balls and cook for another 3-4 minutes. Thicken gravy with tapioca flour blended in 1 tablespoon water. Season to taste, stir in 1 tablespoon oil and serve.

Braised Vegetable Marrow

Preparation : 25 mins.
Cooking   : 40 mins.
Serves   : 4-6

1 large vegetable marrow
½ cup medium-sized prawns
½ teaspoon sugar
1 teaspoon salt
5 Chinese mushrooms
½ cup lean pork
1 chilli
1 tablespoon fish sauce
shake of pepper
oil for deep-fat frying
2 shallots, sliced
1 teaspoon tapioca flour
1 stalk spring onion, chopped

Scrape off the skin of the vegetable marrow, cut it in half down the length and cut each half diagonally into 2 or 3 pieces. Each piece should be about 3 inches (7 ½ cm) long. Shell and devein the prawns, and after cleaning, season with a pinch of sugar and salt. Soak the mushrooms for a few minutes to soften, then wash them. Finely shred mushrooms, pork and chilli. Cut the spring onion into 1 ½ inch (4 cm) lengths. Mix gravy ingredients: in 1 cup water mix salt, fish sauce, sugar and pepper.

Heat the oil for deep-fat frying. Fry the marrow pieces till brown all over. Set aside.

Remove all but 1 tablespoon oil. Brown shallots, then fry pork, mushrooms and prawns till they change colour. Add fried vegetable marrow and the gravy mixture, cover and allow the marrow to simmer slowly till tender, about 30 minutes.

When the marrow is tender, boil quickly to reduce gravy if necessary and then thicken gravy with tapioca flour blended with 1 tablespoon water. Season to taste.

To serve, arrange vegetable marrow pieces, rounded side upwards, on a serving dish and pour gravy over them. Garnish with spring onion and chilli.

Fried Shredded Vegetable Marrow

Preparation : 15 mins.
Cooking   : 10 mins.
Serves   : 4-6

1 vegetable marrow
1 stalk spring onion
15 strands transparent noodles (fun see or
    sohoon)
1 tablespoon dried prawns
4 tablespoons oil
2 shallots, sliced
½ teaspoon salt
½ teaspoon monosodium glutamate
1 teaspoon soy sauce
shake of pepper

Scrape off the skin, then clean and shred the vegetable marrow. Cut spring onion into 1 ½ inch (4 cm) lengths. Soak transparent noodles to soften, then cut into 2 inch (5 cm) lengths. Soak the dried prawns.

Heat the oil, brown sliced shallots and fry dried prawns for 1 minute. Add shredded vegetable marrow, salt and monosodium glutamate and toss all together till well mixed. Add ¼ cup water to the vegetable, cover and cook for 5 minutes.

When the marrow is tender, add transparent noodles and spring onion and stir-fry till well mixed. Season well with soy sauce, stir in 1 tablespoon oil and serve with a good shake of pepper.

Note: Cucumber may be used instead of vegetable marrow.

Chinese White Cabbage with Crab and Egg Sauce

Preparation : 15 mins.
Cooking   : 8-10 mins.
Serves   : 4-6

1⅓ pounds (600 g) Chinese white cabbage
1 cup stock
1 teaspoon salt
½ teaspoon sugar
½ teaspoon sesame oil
shake of pepper
5 tablespoons oil
2 teaspoons fish sauce
2 shallots, sliced
½ cup crabmeat.
1 teaspoon tapioca flour
1 egg, beaten

Discard the old leaves and use only the tender young leaves at the centre of the white cabbage. Wash and cut into 2-inch lengths. Drain. Mix gravy ingredients: to one cup of stock add ½ teaspoon salt, ½ teaspoon sugar, sesame oil and pepper.

Boil 2 cups water with ¼ teaspoon salt in a pan and when it boils put in the white cabbage. Cover and cook for 5 minutes. Rinse vegetables in cold water to stop further cooking and drain well.

Heat 2 tablespoons oil in a pan and toss cabbage in this. Add fish sauce. Arrange cabbage leaves on a serving dish.

Heat another 2 tablespoons oil and brown the shallots. Add the gravy mixture and crab meat. When gravy boils, thicken it with tapioca flour blended with 1 tablespoon water. Season to taste and turn off the heat. Add a beaten egg and 1 tablespoon oil, stir once and pour this gravy over the cabbage. Sprinkle pepper on top and serve at once.

Fried Diced Long Beans

Preparation : 20-25 mins.
Cooking   : 10 mins.
Serves   : 4-6

1 tablespoon preserved radish *(choy poh)*
12 long beans (green variety)
1 piece firm white bean curd
½ cup medium-sized prawns, shelled
5 tablespoons oil
2 shallots, sliced
1 teaspoon soy sauce
½ teaspoon salt
2 tablespoons roasted peanuts
1 chilli, finely chopped
a shake of pepper

Dice preserved radish into ¼ inch (½ cm) cubes and soak in water. Dice the long beans, bean curd and prawns.

Heat 3 tablespoons oil and fry the bean curd till lightly browned. Remove to a dish.

Add another tablespoon of oil to the pan. When it is hot, brown the shallots, then add the prawns and stir-fry till they are cooked. Add preserved radish and long beans and toss all together. Combine soy sauce, salt and about 2 tablespoons water and pour this into the pan. Stir-fry for a few minutes till long beans are cooked. Finally, add the bean curd, peanuts and chilli, and toss to mix well. Season to taste and serve with a good shake of pepper.

Gado-Gado
(Vegetables with Peanut Sauce)

Preparation : 30 mins (for sauce)
10 mins (for vegetables)
Cooking   : 10 mins (for sauce)
10 mins (for vegetables)
Serves   : 4-6

oil for deep-fat frying
2 firm white bean curd squares
1 egg
1 potato
½ cucumber
1 cup bean sprouts
6 cabbage leaves
5 long beans
2 teaspoons salt
1 cup grated coconut
10 red chillies
8 shallots
2 cloves garlic
1 × 1 × ¼ inch (2½ × 2½ × ½ cm) piece
   shrimp paste
1 cup peanuts
1 tablespoon tamarind
6 tablespoons oil
2 tablespoons palm sugar *(gula melaka)*,
   ground

Heat the oil and fry the bean curd till both sides are lightly browned. Remove and drain well. When cool, cut each bean curd square into 10-12 pieces.

Boil the egg and potato and slice them. Shred the cucumber. Remove the brown tails of

bean sprouts, cut cabbage leaves into ½ inch (1 cm) strips, and cut long beans into 1 inch (2½ cm) lengths. Boil 1 cup water with ½ teaspoon salt and cook cabbage and long beans. In the same way, scald bean sprouts. Drain vegetables well.

Arrange the vegetables neatly in small serving bowls and garnish with egg and bean curd slices. Serve with peanut sauce.

Peanut Sauce

Add a little water to the grated coconut and extract 1 cup coconut milk. Pound together chillies, shallots, garlic and shrimp paste till fine. Roast peanuts and coarsely grind them in a mortar. Prepare ¼ cup tamarind juice.

Heat the oil and fry ground ingredients till well cooked. Add palm sugar, coconut milk and 1 teaspoon salt and cook for 3-4 minutes before adding tamarind juice. When gravy is cooked and well blended, add the ground peanuts, season well and serve in a sauce-boat.

Chinese Pickle

Preparation: 30 mins.

1 cucumber
1 small Chinese radish *(lopak)*
1 carrot
1 slice unripe papaya
2 red chillies
1 cup vinegar
2-3 tablespoons sugar
1 tablespoon salt

Clean and cut all vegetables into very thin slices. Sprinkle salt over them, toss to mix and leave for ½ hour.

Wash vegetables to remove salt and press out all the water with a clean, dry tea towel. Leave them on a piece of muslin and allow them to dry in a breezy place for 1 hour.

When they are dry, place all vegetables in a bowl and add vinegar and sugar. Pour in enough vinegar to cover the vegetables. Season pickle to taste, adding more sugar if necessary. Leave pickle for at least 6 hours before serving.

This pickle will keep in a cool place for up to a week, or you can refrigerate it.

Note: Pickled ginger, which is eaten with the Chinese "century eggs", is made the same way.

Masak Lodeh

Preparation: 20-25 mins.
Cooking   : 10-15 mins.
Serves   : 4

¼ **cup shrimps**
4 ounces (120 g) cabbage
4 ounces (120 g) long beans
4 eggplants
2 pieces *tempe*
1 coconut, grated
1 tablespoon oil
2 cloves garlic, sliced
6 shallots, sliced
2 slices galingale
4 red chillies, sliced
1 teaspoon salt, or to taste
1 tablespoon oil

Shell and devein the shrimps. Cut cabbage into ½ inch (1 cm) strips and long beans into 1½ inch (4 cm) lengths. Cut eggplants into 1½ inch (4 cm) pieces, then quarter each piece. Cut *tempe* into ½ inch (1 cm) pieces.

Extract 2 cups coconut milk from the grated coconut.

Heat oil in a pan over medium heat and fry garlic and shallots for 1 minute. Add shrimps and galingale, fry for another minute, then add coconut milk and salt. When coconut milk boils, add chillies, vegetables and *tempe*. Cover the pan and allow coconut milk to come to a boil again.

As soon as coconut milk boils, remove the cover, stir continuously and cook for a further 4-5 minutes or until vegetales are tender. Season to taste and serve with *Lontong*.

Acar Timun
(Cucumber Pickle)

Preparation : 1 hour
Cooking   : 20-25 mins.

2 cucumbers
1 carrot
1 red chilli
1 Bombay onion
2 tablespoons salt
8 dried chillies
8 shallots
4 cloves garlic
¾ inch (2 cm) piece ginger
3 candlenuts
½ cup dried prawns
½ cup oil
½ teaspoon mustard seeds
½ teaspoon turmeric powder
¾ cup vinegar
3½ tablespoons sugar

Cut cucumbers and carrot into 1 inch (2½ cm) fingers. Cut the red chilli into ¼ inch (½ cm) strips and the Bombay onion into ¼ inch (½ cm) wedges. Sprinkle salt over the cut vegetables and let them stand for at least 2 hours. When vegetables are limp, wash away the salt and spread them out on a clean, dry tea towel in a breezy place to dry.

Grind together chillies, shallots, garlic, ginger and candlenuts. Pound dried prawns.

Heat the oil and fry mustard seeds for ½ minute before adding ground ingredients and turmeric powder. Fry for another 3-4 minutes. When the ground ingredients separate from the oil, add the dried prawns and continue cooking for another 2-3 minutes before adding vinegar and sugar. Cook slowly till the mixture is fairly thick. Season with more sugar and salt if necessary.

Stir in the prepared vegetables and toss quickly to mix well. As soon as the vegetables are well-mixed with the spices, remove the pan from heat.

Cool slightly before filling into clean, warm bottles.

Note: It is best to leave the acar for 1 day before serving. Acar Timun keeps very well for a week or more.

Daun Keledek Masak Lemak
(Sweet Potato Greens in Coconut Milk)

Preparation : 30 mins.
Cooking   : 10 mins.
Serves   : 4-6

1 pound (450 g) sweet potato greens
1 sweet potato
1 tablespoon dried prawns
2 red chillies
4 shallots
1 × 1 × ¼ inch (2½ × 2½ × ½ cm) piece
    shrimp paste
½ coconut
3 tablespoons oil
1 teaspoon salt

Clean sweet potato greens and peel tough fibrous skin from the stems cut into 2½ inch (6½ cm) lengths. Peel and cut up sweet potato into 1 inch (2½ cm) cubes. Soak the dried prawns. Pound together chillies, shallots and shrimp paste. Extract ¼ cup first coconut milk and 1 cup second coconut milk.

Heat the oil and fry pounded ingredients for 2-3 minutes till the oil separates from the ingredients. Add the dried prawns and stir-fry for 1 minute before adding salt and the second extraction of coconut milk.

When the mixture boils, add sweet potato cubes and the greens. Cover and cook for 4-5 minutes. When the sweet potato and greens are cooked, add the first extraction of coconut milk. As soon as it boils again, remove from heat. Season to taste and serve.

Note: Spinach, cabbage, *sayur manis* and shredded *chocho* may be substituted for sweet potato greens.

Eggplant with Crab Sauce

Preparation : 10 mins.
Cooking   : 25 mins.
Serves   : 4-6

5 eggplants
1 tablespoon fish sauce
1 tablespoon vinegar
1 teaspoon sugar
4 tablespoons oil
2 cloves garlic, chopped
½ cup crabmeat
½ teaspoon tapioca flour
shake of pepper
1 chilli, shredded

Grill the eggplants till they are soft and cooked. Skin them and cut them into halves lengthwise and cut each length into quarters. Lay the pieces on a serving dish. Mix gravy ingredients: in 1 cup water mix fish sauce, vinegar and sugar.

Heat the oil and brown the garlic. Add the gravy mixture and then the crabmeat. When the gravy boils, thicken it with tapioca flour blended with 1 tablespoon water. Season gravy to taste and pour it over the eggplant. Sprinkle a good shake of pepper over the gravy and garnish with shredded chilli before serving.

Note: Eggplants can be boiled instead of grilled, if desired.

Fried Bean Sprouts with Prawns

Preparation : 30 mins.
Cooking   : 5-7 mins.
Serves   : 4-6

10 ounces (300 g) bean sprouts
1 piece firm white bean curd
1 chilli
1 stalk spring onion
10 ounces (300 g) prawns
½ teaspoon sugar
1 teaspoon salt
½ teaspoon tapioca flour
1 teaspoon soy sauce
shake of pepper
4 tablespoons oil
2 shallots, sliced

Remove the brown tails of the bean sprouts. Shred the bean curd and chilli. Cut the spring onion into 1½ inch (4 cm) lengths. Shell the prawns and slit them down the back. Devein them, then wash and season with ¼ teaspoon sugar and ½ teaspoon salt.

Mix gravy ingredients: to 3 tablespoons water add ½ teaspoon tapioca flour, 1 teaspoon soy sauce, ½ teaspoon salt, ¼ teaspoon sugar and a good shake of pepper. Mix well.

Heat 4 tablespoons oil and fry bean curd till firm. Remove to a dish. Brown the sliced shallots and fry prawns in the same oil for 1 minute. Add bean sprouts, bean curd, spring onion, chilli and 1 tablespoon water. Stir-fry for ½ minute. Add the gravy mixture. When it thickens, season to taste and serve at once.

Note: Do not cover the pan to cook bean sprouts as it requires very little cooking. Well-cooked bean sprouts should be firm and crisp.

Fried Eggplant

Preparation: 10 mins.
Cooking   : 10 mins.
Serves   : 4-6

2 eggplants
10 peppercorns
2 teaspoons salt
6-8 tablespoons oil

Pound peppercorns with salt till both are very fine. Slice eggplants diagonally into ½ inch (1 cm) slices and score both sides of each slice lightly. Rub salt and pepper mixture into the scored surfaces. Leave the eggplant to season for 10-15 minutes.

Heat the oil and fry eggplant slices until evenly browned on both sides and cooked. Serve neatly arranged on a flat dish.

Kerabu Timun (Cucumber and Dried Prawn Salad)

Preparation : 20 mins.
Serves   : 6-8

2 cucumbers
1 tablespoon dried prawns
1 × 1 × ¼ inch (2½ × 2½ × ½ cm) piece
   shrimp paste
3 red chillies
 6 shallots, sliced
3 limes
½ teaspoon salt
½ teaspoon sugar

Skin and quarter the cucumbers. Cut away the soft centre and slice each quarter. Wash dried prawns and pound them.

Grill shrimp paste till it is brown on both sides. Pound chillies and grilled shrimp paste to make *sambal blacan.*

Place sliced shallots in a large bowl and squeeze lime juice over them. Add the *sambal blacan* then the dried prawns, sliced cucumber, salt and sugar. Toss together to mix well, season to taste and serve.

Note: Substitute pineapple for cucumber for a sweet-sour salad.

Kerabu Kobis

Preparation : 30 mins.
Cooking   : 10-15 mins.
Serves   : 4-6

1 × 1 × ¼ inch (2½ × 2½ × ½ cm) piece
   shrimp paste
3 red chillies
10 ounces (300 g) cabbage
10 ounces (300 g) small prawns
½ coconut, grated
1½ teaspoons salt
6 shallots, sliced
3 limes

Grill or roast shrimp paste and pound it with red chillies to get *sambal blacan.* Cut cabbage into ½ inch (1 cm) strips. Shell, devein and dice the prawns. Extract first coconut milk from the grated coconut.

Boil 1 cup water with ½ teaspoon salt in a pan. When the water boils, put in the cabbage. Remove cabbage as soon as water boils again. Drain well.

Put coconut milk to boil in a small saucepan and allow it to simmer slowly till it thickens. When it begins to thicken, add prawns to it and cook together till it thickens again. Stir the mixture occasionally to prevent burning.

Squeeze lime juice over sliced shallots and work in the *sambal blacan.* Add boiled cabbage and 1 teaspoon salt and mix well together. Stir the coconut gravy into this cabbage mixture, season to taste and serve.

Fried Mee - Cantonese Style

Recipe: p. 91

Laksa Assam

Recipe: p. 92

Tophats

Recipe: p. 128

Poh Piah

Recipe: p. 122

Pecal

Preparation : 1 hour.
Cooking   : 20 minutes.
Serves   : 4-6

6 ounces (180 g) sweet potato greens
6 ounces (180 g) spinach
5 long beans
6 cabbage leaves
1 teaspoon salt
15 dried chillies
6 shallots
½ cup peanuts
1 tablespoon tamarind (levelled)
2 tablespoons flour
1 cup oil
1 × 1 × ¼ inch (2½ × 2½ × ½ cm) piece
**   shrimp paste**
5 tablespoons palm sugar

Peel fibrous skin from the sweet potato greens. Cut sweet potato greens, spinach and long beans into 2½ inch (6½ cm) lengths and tear cabbage into bite-sized pieces. Boil the vegetables with a little salt till cooked, then drain them well and set aside.

Clean the chillies and shallots, dry thoroughly. Roast 1 cup peanuts. Remove seeds from the tamarind and press the pulp together into a cake.

Mix 2 tablespoons flour with about 8 tablespoons water to get a very thin batter. (Add the water a little at a time till the consistency is about right). Mix in ½ cup peanuts.

Heat the cup of oil in a pan. When it is hot, ladle out the peanut in batter mixture a tablespoon at a time and gently drop at the edge of the hot oil so that it forms a thin wafer. Fry till the wafers are brown and crisp. Remove and drain well.

Using the same oil, fry the dried chillies, shallots and tamarind separately: first fry the chillies for about ¼ minute till lightly browned, then remove and fry the shallots till cooked; dish out the shallots and fry the tamarind for about 1 minute. Remove all but 1 tablespoon oil and fry the shrimp paste till it is cooked. Lastly, toss the remaining 1 cup of roasted peanuts in the oily pan till peanuts are coated with oil.

Pound together till fine the fried chillies, shallots, shrimp paste, tamarind and peanuts. When ingredients are well pounded, add palm sugar and salt.

To make Pecal gravy mix the pounded ingredients with a little boiled water. Serve the gravy with boiled vegetables and crispy peanut wafers.

Note: Pecal gravy made this way and refrigerated can keep for months. When required, mix as much as desired with a little warm water and serve it with any variety of leafy vegetable. The amount of water added depends on the desired consistency.

Sambal Kelapa

Preparation: 10 mins.
Cooking   : 10-15 mins.

½ red chilli
3 shallots
1 thin slice galingale
½ teaspoon salt
1 tablespoon oil
6 tablespoons grated coconut

Pound together chilli, shallots, galingale and salt. Heat oil in a pan over medium heat and fry these ingredients for 1 or 2 minutes. Add coconut and fry all together, stirring constantly till the coconut is dry and light brown.

Cool and store in a dry bottle till required.

Soups

Steamed Melon Soup

Preparation : 30-35 mins.
Cooking : 1½ hours
Serves : 4-6

1 Chinese winter melon, about 6 pounds
  (3 kg)
3 tablespoons lotus seeds
1 cup chicken meat, diced
4 Chinese mushrooms, diced
½ cup button mushrooms
½ inch (1 cm) piece ginger, sliced
5 cups chicken stock
2 teaspoons salt

Slice a piece about 1 inch (2½ cm) thick from the top of the melon. With a tablespoon, scoop out the soft centre of the melon so that a melon bowl is obtained. The hollow should have a capacity of about 8 cups. The top of the melon bowl could be decorated by serrating the edge. Place the melon bowl in a large pan of boiling water, enough to cover the melon completely. Cover and cook over low heat for 20 minutes. Remove the melon and plunge it into a basin of cold water to cool.

Drain well and stand melon bowl firmly in a heatproof bowl.

Soak the lotus seeds in cold water overnight to soften. Boil them for ½ hour till tender. Leave in cold water to cool, then peel off the skin, and with the help of a toothpick, push out the shoot from the top. These are tedious but necessary tasks as the brown skin would discolour the soup and the embryo is dreadfully bitter.

Place chicken meat, Chinese mushrooms, button mushrooms, lotus seeds and ginger in the melon and add enough stock to fill slightly more than ¾ of the melon. Add salt and steam melon for 1½ hours. Season to taste and serve.

Chicken and Corn Soup

Preparation : 15 mins.
Cooking : 8-10 mins.
Serves : 4-6

5 ounces (150 g) chicken meat
1 egg white
3 cups chicken stock
1 tin creamed sweetcorn
2 teaspoons salt
1 teaspoon soy sauce
1 teaspoon sesame oil
shake of pepper
3 tablespoons oil
2 tablespoons cornflour

Mince chicken meat and mix it well with egg white and 3 tablespoons water.

Pour the stock into a large bowl and stir

creamed corn into it. Add salt, soy sauce, sesame oil and pepper to season the mixture.

In a saucepan, heat 3 tablespoons oil and pour in the seasoned corn mixture. Allow the mixture to boil for about 3 minutes. Thicken the soup by adding cornflour blended with 3 tablespoons water, stirring all the while to prevent lumps forming. When soup is thick and boiling, stir in chicken meat. Remove soup from heat as soon as it boils again. Season and serve with a good shake of pepper.

Note: If desired, crabmeat may be added to this soup.

Watercress and Pork Soup

Preparation : 15 mins.
Cooking   : 1½ hours.
Serves   : 4-6

10 ounces (300 g) shoulder pork
1⅓ pounds (600 g) watercress
1 teaspoon soy sauce
1 teaspoon salt

Clean the piece of pork, cutting away excess fat. Clean watercress and pluck off all green leaves and young shoots, leaving only the stems.

Place the piece of pork in a saucepan with 6 cups water and bring it to a boil. Then add watercress stems (usually bound together with a piece of clean thread for easy removal later) and allow soup to simmer for 1-1½ hours.

When the soup is ready, take out the piece of pork and slice it into ¼ inch (½ cm) slices. Remove watercress stems and throw them away. Bring soup to a boil again and add salt, watercress shoots and leaves. As soon as the soup boils again, remove it from heat and season to taste.

Take out watercress shoots and lay them on a serving dish. Arrange sliced pork on top and sprinkle soy sauce and pepper over it before serving. Serve soup separately.

Note: If desired, add 2 preserved duck's gizzards to the soup and boil them with the pork. As the gizzards are salty, taste before adding salt to the soup.

Sweet Sour Soup

Preparation : 20 mins.
Cooking   : 10 mins.
Serves   : 4-6

3 pieces "wood ear" fungus (mok yee)
4 ounces (120 g) lean pork
1 slice ham or 2 rashers bacon
1 piece soft white bean curd
3 Chinese mushrooms
2 stalks spring onion
½ inch (1 cm) piece ginger
2 tablespoons cornflour
1½ teaspoons soy sauce
¼ teaspoon pepper
2 tablespoons vinegar
1 teaspoon sesame oil
4 cups stock
½ teaspoon salt
½ teaspoon sugar
1 egg

Soak "wood ear" fungus to soften then clean and shred them. Shred the pork, ham or bacon, bean curd, mushrooms, spring onions and ginger.

Marinate pork in a mixture of 1 teaspoon cornflour, ½ teaspoon soy sauce and a shake of pepper. Mix 1 teaspoon soy sauce, the vinegar and sesame oil, a good shake of pepper and the shredded spring onion and ginger in a large soup bowl.

Place stock, salt and sugar in a saucepan and bring it to a boil. When the soup boils, add "wood ears", bean curd, mushrooms, ham or bacon and allow it to boil for 2 minutes. Add the seasoned pork, stirring to separate the shreds. When the soup boils again, thicken it by adding the remaining cornflour blended with 3 tablespoons water. As soon as the soup boils again, turn off the heat.

Add a beaten egg slowly to the hot soup, stirring gently, then pour the soup over the seasoning in the soup bowl. Stir gently to mix, season to taste and serve at once.

Beef Soup

Preparation : 15-20 mins.
Cooking   : 8-10 mins.
Serves   : 4

10 ounces (300 g) beef steak
1 teaspoon tapioca flour
2 teaspoons soy sauce
¾ teaspoon salt
shake of pepper
2 pieces soft bean curd
2 tablespoons oil
2 shallots, sliced
2 tablespoons green peas
1 stalk spring onion, chopped
a shake of pepper

Clean and slice steak very thinly and season with tapioca flour, soy sauce, salt and pepper for at least 20 minutes. Clean and cut each piece of bean curd into 8-10 pieces.

Heat 2 tablespoons oil in a saucepan and brown the shallots. Add 3 cups water to browned shallots. When it comes to a boil, add ½ teaspoon salt, bean curd and green peas and allow them to boil together for 3 minutes. When peas are cooked, add the steak, stirring to separate the slices. As soon as the soup boils again, add chopped spring onion and remove from heat at once. Season to taste and serve with a good shake of pepper.

Note: As a quick one-dish meal, serve this soup with some rice vermicelli *(mee hoon)* or transparent noodles *(fun see* or *sohoon).* Soak the noodles in cold water to soften. Add rice vermicelli or transparent noodles with the steak. If desired, Chinese white cabbage or mustard greens may be used to substitute for green peas.

Beef and Radish Soup

Preparation : 10 mins.
Cooking   : 1½ hours
Serves   : 4

10 ounces (300 g) beef flank
1 Chinese radish
10 peppercorns
1 segment star anise
1 teaspoon salt
1 tablespoon soy sauce
shake of pepper
2 teaspoons chopped spring onion

Clean and cut beef into 1½ inch (4 cm) cubes. Halve the radish lengthwise and cut each half diagonally into 1 inch (2½ cm) pieces.

Put beef, radish, peppercorns and star anise with 6 cups water into a saucepan and let it come to a boil. When soup boils, lower heat and allow it to simmer for at least 1½ hours.

When the soup is ready, it should have about 4 cups water. Season with salt, soy sauce and pepper and serve garnished with spring onion.

Pork, Liver and Chinese Spinach Soup

Preparation : 15 mins.
Cooking   : 10 mins.
Serves   : 4-6

2 slices ginger
4 ounces (120 g) lean pork
1 teaspoon tapioca flour
1½ teaspoons soy sauce
shake of pepper
3 ounces (90 g) pig's liver
½ teaspoon salt
3 tablespoons oil
2 shallots, sliced
8 ounces (225 g) Chinese spinach *(tong hoe)*

Pound the ginger slices and extract juice. Slice the pork thinly and season with ½ teaspoon tapioca flour, ½ teaspoon soy sauce and a shake of pepper. Slice the liver and season with ½ teaspoon tapioca flour, ginger juice and ¼ teaspoon salt.

Heat 3 tablespoons oil and brown the shallots. Add 4 cups water, 1 teaspoon soy sauce and ¼ teaspoon salt. When the water boils, add pork slices, stirring to separate them. Cover and allow pork to cook for 3 minutes before adding spinach and liver. Cover and allow the soup to boil for another 2 minutes. Remove from heat, season to taste and serve with a good shake of pepper.

Pork Balls and Bean Curd Soup

Preparation : 45 mins.
Cooking   : 20 mins.
Serves   : 4-6

½ pound (225 g) shoulder pork
½ cup shrimps, shelled
1 teaspoon tapioca flour
1 teaspoon salt
½ teaspoon sesame oil
shake of pepper
1 egg white
2 pieces soft bean curd
4 Chinese cabbage leaves
3 tablespoons oil
3 cloves garlic, chopped
2 shallots, sliced
1 teaspoon soy sauce
1 teaspoon fish sauce

Mince the pork and shrimps. Mix together pork, prawns, tapioca flour, salt, sesame oil, a good shake of pepper and the egg white. Knead the ingredients together to mix well, then shape into balls.

Clean the bean curd and cut into 1 inch (2½ cm) cubes. Cut the Chinese cabbage into 1 inch (2½ cm) wide pieces.

Heat 3 tablespoons oil in a saucepan and brown the garlic. Remove to a small dish.

Brown shallots and add 4 cups water combined with soy sauce and fish sauce. When the water boils, add the meat balls and allow them to cook for 2-3 minutes. When meat balls are cooked, add Chinese cabbage and bean curd. Allow the soup to simmer for another 3 minutes before turning off the heat and seasoning to taste. Serve the soup sprinkled with browned garlic.

Note: If desired, preserved cabbage *(tong choy)* can be added to this soup.

Dumpling Soup (Wonton Soup)

Preparation : 30 mins.
Cooking   : 10 mins.
Serves   : 4-6

5 ounces (150 g) small prawns
½ teaspoon sugar
½ teaspoon salt
5 ounces (150 g) mustard greens *(choy sum)*
½ inch (1 cm) piece ginger
¼ cup minced pork
shake of pepper
25-30 *wonton* **skins**
4 cups stock
2 teaspoons fish sauce
½ teaspoon sesame oil
2-3 teaspoons chopped spring onion

Shell and devein prawns. Season them with ½ teaspoon sugar and ¼ teaspoon salt for about 20 minutes, then rinse under a running tap and drain well. Chop the prawns coarsely.

Clean and pluck mustard greens into 2 inch (5 cm) lengths. Cut off 2 thin slices of ginger and pound the rest to extract ginger juice.

Season chopped prawns and minced pork with ¼ teaspoon salt, ginger juice and a good shake of pepper. Spread out each *wonton* skin and place a teaspoon of the filling in the centre. Fold *wonton* skin over diagonally so that the opposite corners meet. Make another fold just below the filling to enable the folded corners to be drawn together. With a drop of water, press to seal the folded corners together.

In a saucepan boil stock, ginger slices, fish sauce and a good shake of pepper (season soup to taste).

In another saucepan boil 4 cups water. When the water boils, add *wonton* and mustard greens. Cover and cook for 2 minutes. When a *wonton* is cooked, it floats. Drain cooked *wonton* and greens and place them in a serving soup bowl. Sprinkle sesame oil over the *wontons* and pour boiling soup over them. Garnish with chopped spring onion and a good shake of pepper and serve at once.

Fish Ball Soup

Preparation : 30 mins.
Cooking   : 40 mins.
Serves   : 4-6

10 ounces (300 g) Spanish mackerel *(ikan tenggiri)*
1 teaspoon tapioca flour
1½ teaspoons salt
5 ounces (150 g) mustard greens *(choy sum)*
10 strands transparent noodles *(fun see or sohoon)*
1 teaspoon preserved cabbage *(tong choy)*
4 tablespoons oil
2 cloves garlic, chopped
¼ inch (½ cm) piece ginger, sliced
1 tablespoon soy sauce
shake of pepper

Clean and fillet the fish and scrape off the flesh with tablespoon. Knead the flesh well on a chopping board with the flat side of a kitchen knife until it is smooth. Add tapioca flour and 1 teaspoon salt and work it in with 4-5 tablespoons water until the flesh is a soft and sticky paste. Wet hands in salt water and shape fish balls. Dip each fish ball in salt water before placing it on a plate to prevent them from sticking together.

Pluck mustard greens into 2 inch (5 cm) lengths, soak transparent noodles in water and wash preserved cabbage.

Heat the oil in a saucepan and brown the garlic. Remove to a small dish.

Lightly brown the ginger slices in hot oil and fry fish bones and skin for about 2 minutes before adding 4 cups water and ½ teaspoon salt. Simmer for at least 30 minutes to get a good fish stock.

Strain the fish stock, return it to the saucepan and allow it to come to a boil before adding fish balls. When the soup boils again and fish balls are floating, add mustard greens, transparent noodles and preserved cabbage.

As soon as it boils, remove from heat, season it well with soy sauce, salt and pepper and serve it with browned garlic sprinkled on top.

Szechuan Vegetable and Pork Soup

Preparation : 20 mins.
Cooking   : 15 mins.
Serves   : 4-6

5 ounces (150 g) lean pork
1 teaspoon tapioca flour
1 teaspoon soy sauce
shake of pepper
1 stalk spring onion
½ cup Szechuan vegetable, sliced
½ teaspoon sesame oil

Clean and slice pork thinly. Season pork slices with tapioca flour, soy sauce and a little pepper. Cut the spring onion into 1½ inch (4 cm) lengths.

Heat 4 cups water in a saucepan. When the water boils, add Szechuan vegetable slices and allow it to boil for about 4 minutes. Add the sliced pork, stirring to separate the slices. When pork has been boiled for 2-3 minutes, add sesame oil and turn off the heat. Season to taste, add spring onion and serve with a good shake of pepper.

Noodles

Fried Hokkien Mee

Preparation : 20 mins.
Cooking   : 10-15 mins.
Serves   : 4

4 ounces (100 g) pork
6 ounces (150 g) medium-sized prawns
3 medium-sized squids (optional)
4 stalks mustard greens *(choy sum)*
1 tablespoon black soy sauce
1 tablespoon soy sauce
½ teaspoon sugar
½ teaspoon salt
5 tablespoons oil
6 cloves garlic, chopped
1⅓ pounds (600 g) thick noodles
shake of pepper

Slice pork, shell and devein prawns, clean squids (if used) and cut them into ½ inch (1 cm) slices. Clean and pluck mustard greens into 1½ inch (4 cm) lengths. Mix black soy sauce, soy sauce, sugar and salt in 1 cup water for a gravy mixture.

Heat oil in a pan and brown the garlic. Add pork and fry for a minute till it changes colour, then add prawns and squids and fry for another minute before adding the gravy mixture.

When the gravy mixture boils, add mustard greens and then the noodles. Mix well and keep turning the noodles over till most of the gravy is absorbed. Season to taste and serve with a good shake of pepper.

Serve fried Hokkien mee with either fresh sliced chillies in soy sauce or *sambal blacan*.

Note: The following substitutions may be made: rice vermicelli or rice noodles *(kway teow)* for Hokkien mee or thick noodles; and cabbage for mustard greens. Mussels may also be added to this dish. Sometimes Hokkien Mee is served with a slight well in the centre and a raw egg is broken into this well. The heat from the noodles below cooks the egg very lightly.

Kuih Rose

Recipe: p. 109

Shanghai Pancakes

Recipe: p. 120

Pineapple Tarts

Recipe: p. 106

Curry Puffs

Recipe: p. 109

Fried Mee-Cantonese Style

Preparation : 20-25 mins.
Cooking   : 10-15 mins.
Serves   : 1-2

4 medium-sized freshwater prawns
6 ounces (150 g) lean pork
4 ounces (100 g) pig's liver
4 ounces (100 g) threadfin *(ikan kurau)*
6 stalks mustard greens *(choy sum)*
2 teaspoons tapioca flour
½ teaspoon salt
2 teaspoons soy sauce
shake of pepper
¼ teaspoon sugar
½ teaspoon sesame oil
1 piece fried egg noodles of about 10 inches
    (25 cm) in diameter and 8 ounces (225 g) in
    weight
½ cup oil
3 shallots, sliced
2 cloves garlic, chopped
1 egg

Wash the prawns and halve them lengthwise. Slice pork, liver and fish. Use only the young shoots of mustard greens and leave them whole. Season pork with ½ teaspoon soy sauce and a shake of pepper. Season liver with ½ teaspoon tapioca flour, ½ teaspoon soy sauce and a shake of pepper.

Mix ingredients for gravy: to 1 cup water add 1 teaspoon soy sauce, ¼ teaspoon salt, ¼ teaspoon sugar, ½ teaspoon sesame oil and a good shake of pepper.

Place dried egg noodles in a large bowl and pour boiling water over it. As soon as noodles appear limp, drain well. Heat 2 tablespoons oil and fry softened noodles for 3-4 minutes. Lay noodles on a serving dish, spreading out as flat as possible.

Heat 3 tablespoons oil and brown the shallots and garlic. Add prawns and pork and fry for a minute till the colour changes. Add the gravy mixture, cover and cook for 3-4 minutes. Add mustard greens, liver and fish and as soon as the gravy boils again, thicken with 1 teaspoon tapioca flour blended with ¼ cup water.

Season gravy to taste and turn off the heat.

Beat the egg and add it to the gravy. Mix in 1 tablespoon oil and then pour gravy over the fried noodles. Sprinkle with pepper and serve with pickled chillies.

Note: Any kind of meat can substitute for pork and liver and any other seafood may be used in place of prawns and threadfin.

Vegetarian Rice Vermicelli

Preparation : 25 mins.
Cooking   : 20 mins.
Serves   : 4

4 Chinese mushrooms
1 bundle (about 8 ounces or 225 g) rice
    vermicelli *(meehoon)*
3 cabbage leaves
1 carrot
1 piece firm white bean curd
3 pieces *teem chok* (hard bean curd squares)
1 chilli
4 stalks mustard greens *(choy sum)*
1 sprig spring onion
7 tablespoons oil
½ teaspoon salt
1 tablespoon soy sauce
1 teaspoon monosodium glutamate
1 cup bean sprouts

Soak mushrooms in water and wash rice vermicelli. Shred cabbage leaves, carrot, bean curd, mushrooms, *teem chok* and chilli. Cut mustard greens and spring onion into 1 ½ inch (4 cm) lengths.

Heat 4 tablespoons oil and fry the bean curd till firm. Dish it out and drain. Fry *teem chok* over a very low fire till lightly browned. Remove to a dish.

Add another 3 tablespoons oil to the pan and fry the cabbage, mushroom and carrot shreds, and the mustard greens, fried *teem chok* and rice vermicelli together. Add salt, soy sauce and monosodium glutamate to the rice vermicelli and stir to mix thoroughly. Add a little water now and then if the rice vermicelli appears stiff.

See that the ingredients are well mixed and cooked. Cooked rice vermicelli is limp, yet retains its fineness, but overcooked rice vermicelli expands and is "mushy". Add the bean sprouts and the spring onion. Toss for a minute to mix well and to cook the vegetables. Season and serve garnished with chilli shreds.

Laksa Assam

Preparation : 40-45 mins.
Cooking   : 20-25 mins.
Serves   : 2

1⅓ pounds (600 g) mackerel *(ikan kembong)*
15 red chillies
15 shallots
2 stalks lemon grass
1 × 1 × ¼ inch (2½ × 2½ × ½ cm) piece
    shrimp paste
1 bundle (about 8 ounces or 225 g) thick rice
    vermicelli
½ cucumber
1 slice pineapple
1 *bunga kantan*
2 limes
1 onion
1 cup mint leaves
6 pieces *assam gelugur*
1 bundle (about a handful) *daun kessom*
1½ teaspoons salt
1 tablespoon prawn paste

Boil the fish in 6 cups water till cooked. Remove the bones and flake the flesh. Grind together 13 chillies, shallots, lemon grass and shrimp paste. Soak the rice vermicelli for about 30 minutes. Shred the cucumber, pine-apple slice and *bunga kantan*. Slice the remaining 2 chillies. Cut limes into wedges. Halve the onion and slice each half very finely into half-rings. Pluck mint leaves from their stalks.

Add the ground ingredients, *assam gelugur, daun kessom* and salt to the fish stock and let it simmer for 10-15 minutes. Season to taste and return flaked fish to the gravy.

Boil the rice vermicelli for 10-15 minutes till softened. Drain well.

Arrange the cucumber, pineapple, *bunga kantan,* onion, chilli, mint leaves and limes in a flat dish. Put equal portions of rice vermicelli in 6 Chinese serving bowls and pour boiling gravy over it. Serve with the plate of garnishing and prawn paste mixed with 2 tablespoons water in a separate bowl.

Laksa Lemak

Preparation : 1 hour.
Cooking   : 30 mins.
Serves   : 4

2 pounds (900 g) herring *(ikan parang)* or
    mackerel *(ikan kembong* or *ikan tenggiri)*
1 bundle (about 8 ounces or 225 g) thick rice
    vermicelli
½ coconut, grated
1 stalk lemon grass
10 shallots
6 peppercorns
1 × 1 × ¼ inch (2½ × 2½ × ½ cm) piece
    shrimp paste
½ cucumber
1 red chilli
1 slice pineapple
5 *daun limau perut* (optional)
1 cup mint leaves
2 limes
7 tablespoons oil
1½ tablespoons curry powder
1½ teaspoons salt

Clean the fish. Soak rice vermicelli for 30 minutes before boiling. Extract ½ cup first coconut milk and 4 cups second coconut milk. Grind the lemon grass, shallots, peppercorns and shrimp paste. Shred the cucumber, chilli, pineapple slice and *daun limau perut.* Pluck mint leaves from the stalks and cut limes into wedges.

Heat 7 tablespoons oil and fry the ground ingredients and the curry powder for about 5 minutes. Add the second extraction of coconut milk and the salt. When it boils, add the cleaned fish. Allow the fish to cook slowly for 10 minutes. When it is cooked, take it out, remove all the bones and flake off the flesh. Return flaked fish and add *daun limau perut* to the gravy and cook for another 2 minutes. Add the first lot of coconut milk and when it comes to a boil, turn off the heat at once. Season to taste before serving.

Drain the soaked rice vermicelli and put it into boiling water to boil for 15 minutes or until limp. Drain well.

Arrange the cucumber, pineapple and chilli shreds and the lime wedges and mint leaves on a plate. Put equal portions of rice vermicelli into 6 Chinese serving bowls and pour boiling gravy over it.

Note: For Curry *Mee* use 1⅓ pounds (600 g) cockles, ½ pound (225 g) medium-sized prawns and ¼ chicken cut into small pieces instead of fish. Also add 4 squares of fried bean curd to the curry. The more commonly used fine vermicelli, thick yellow noodles or spaghetti could be used in place of thick rice vermicelli.

Wonton Mee

Preparation : 40 mins.
Cooking   : 20 mins.
Serves   : 4

1 tablespoon water chestnuts *or* yam bean
½ inch (1 cm) piece ginger
6 ounces (150 g) mustard greens *(choy sum)*
12 ounces (300 g) Chinese roast pork *(char siew)*
6 ounces (150 g) minced pork
2 teaspoons chopped spring onion
1 teaspoon tapioca flour
1 teaspoon salt
3 teaspoons soy sauce
3 teaspoons sesame oil
1 egg white
shake of pepper
25 wonton skins
5 tablespoons oil
3 shallots, sliced
6 cups stock
4 teaspoons oyster sauce
4 bundles (about 12 ounces or 350 g) fresh fine
    egg noodles

Dice water chestnuts or yam bean finely. Cut off 2 thin slices of ginger and pound the rest to extract ginger juice. Pluck young shoots of mustard greens and leave them whole. Cut Chinese roast pork into ½ (1 cm) slices.

Mix minced pork with water chestnuts or yam bean, ginger juice, spring onions, tapioca flour, ½ teaspoon salt, 1 teaspoon soy sauce, ½ teaspoon sesame oil, egg white and a good shake of pepper. Knead well to mix the ingredients thoroughly. Spread out a wonton skin and place a teaspoon of this filling in the centre. Press wonton skin together to enclose filling completely.

Heat 2 tablespoons oil and brown the shallot and ginger slices. Add the stock with ½ teaspoon salt, 2 teaspoons soy sauce and a good shake of pepper. Keep the stock hot.

In a saucepan boil 12 cups water. When it boils, add the wontons, cover and cook for 4 minutes till they float. Lift the cooked wontons from boiling water and plunge them into a basin of cold water. Drain well and keep aside.

Prepare 4 serving bowls: in each bowl, place ¼ tablespoon vegetable oil, ¼ teaspoon sesame oil, ½ teaspoon oyster sauce, ¼ teaspoon soy sauce and a shake of pepper.

Allow the water in the saucepan to come to a boil again. Loosen the strands of the 4 bundles of noodles and drop one bundle into the boiling water. Stir with chopsticks and cook for 2 minutes till the noodles float. Use a large slotted spoon to lift the noodles from boiling water and plunge them, still in the spoon, into a basin of cold water. Remove, shake out excess water and plunge into the boiling water again. Lift out at once, drain well and place in one of the 4 prepared serving bowls. Use a pair of chopsticks or a fork to mix in the seasoning thoroughly.

Boil the mustard greens lightly in boiling stock. When cooked, remove to a dish.

To serve, place a quarter portion of mustard greens, wontons and sliced roast pork over the noodles in each bowl before pouring boiling stock over. Serve with pickled green chillies.

Note: Instead of roast pork, other meats may be used. Cooked egg noodles must be plunged into cold water to stop further cooking. If this is not done, the noodles become very soft and starchy. If fresh egg noodles are not available, use approximately 10 ounces (300 g) dried egg noodles. Cook exactly as for fresh noodles but double the cooking time.

Har Mee (Egg noodles with Prawns)

Preparation : 1 hour.
Cooking   : 1½ hours.
Serves   : 6

1⅓ pounds (600 g) spareribs
10 ounces (300 g) lean pork
10 ounces (300 g) medium-sized prawns
1 dried sole
1 teaspoon salt
2 teaspoons soy sauce
5 tablespoons oil
½ cup shallots, sliced
1 tablespoon ground chilli
5 ounces (150 g) bean sprouts
10 ounces (300 g) water convolvulus
    (kangkong)
1⅓ pounds (600 g) thick yellow noodles

Put spareribs in a saucepan with 6 cups water to boil. When it boils, add the lean pork. As soon as it comes to a boil again, lower the heat and allow the soup to simmer for 1-1½ hours. Take out the lean pork after ½ hour and let it cool before slicing. Dish out the spareribs.

Bring the stock to a boil again and put in the prawns. After about 3 minutes, when they should be cooked, take out the prawns and shell them. Halve shelled prawns lengthwise. Return the prawn shells and bones of the dried sole to the stock and let it simmer for another 30 minutes. Strain it, allow it to boil again, then season to taste with salt and soy sauce.

Heat the oil and brown sliced shallots. Remove to a small bowl. Fry the deboned sole over a slow fire till it is brown and crisp. Remove from the pan and pound it till fine.

Mix ground chilli with sufficient water to make a paste. Fry this paste in the same oil used for frying shallots and sole, adding more oil if necessary, till chilli is dark. Remove it to a small dish. In the same pan, fry sliced prawns for 2 minutes till they curl up and are evenly coated with chilli oil.

Remove the brown tails of bean sprouts. Clean and pluck water convolvulus into 2 inch (5 cm) lengths. Boil 3 cups water in a pan and when it boils, scald bean sprouts, followed by the noodles. Drain well. Lastly, boil water convolvulus lightly.

Divide ingredients into 4-6 equal portions for 4-6 bowls. Place bean sprouts, water convolvulus, noodles, pork slices and prawns in this order in each bowl, ladle boiling soup over the ingredients and garnish with powdered sole and browned shallots. Serve prawn noodles with chilli *sambal.*

Note: Instead of noodles alone, rice vermicelli *(meehoon)* or a mixture of noodles and rice vermicelli may be used. The spareribs can be served with the noodles. If a more flavoured soup is desired, pound the prawn shells after shelling the prawns, place the pounded shells in a sieve and stand the sieve in a bowl containing a little water. Rub as much of the pounded shells through as possible. Add this liquid to the soup to "thicken" it. Some people find this too "fishy" for their taste.

Mee Rebus

Preparation : 1 hour.
Cooking   : 2 hours.
Serves   : 4

1 tablespoon coriander
15 dried chillies
20 shallots
1⅓ pounds (600 g) sweet potatoes
2 eggs
2 tomatoes
2 limes
1 tablespoon tamarind
1⅓ pounds (600 g) lean beef
2 cloves
2 inch (5 cm) piece cinnamon bark
2 teaspoons salt
6 tablespoons oil
2 pieces firm white bean curd
1 cup bean sprouts
1⅓ pounds (600 g) thick yellow noodles
2 green chillies, sliced
2-3 teaspoons chopped spring onion

Roast the coriander seeds in a pan over low heat and pound it till fine. Grind together dried chillies and 10 shallots. Boil the sweet potatoes and eggs. Slice the remaining shallots, quarter the tomatoes and cut the limes into wedges. Add ½ cup water to the tamarind to extract tamarind juice.

Boil the beef in 6 cups water. When it boils, lower the heat and allow it to simmer for 1-1½ hours till the beef is tender, then remove it and cut into small slices when cool.

To 5 cups of beef stock, add the ground ingredients, cloves and cinnamon and allow the stock to boil gently for about 10 minutes. While it is boiling, mash the sweet potatoes. Add mashed sweet potatoes, salt and tamarind juice to the gravy. Cook till fairly thick, then season to taste.

Heat 6 tablespoons oil and fry the bean curd till brown on the outside. Remove it to a cutting board and cut each piece into 8 pieces. Brown the sliced shallots and keep for garnishing. Shell and slice the eggs.

Boil 2 cups water and blanch the bean sprouts and then scald the noodles. Drain well.

Lay equal amounts of blanched bean sprouts in 4 serving bowls. Spread the noodles over bean sprouts. Lay sliced meat over the noodles and pour boiling gravy over them. Garnish with sliced egg, bean curd, tomato slices, browned shallots, green chilli and spring onion on top. Serve mee rebus with the lime wedges and gravy.

Mee Siam

Preparation: 25 mins.
Cooking   : 20-25 mins.
Serves   : 4

4 dried chillies
10 shallots
6 stalks chives *(kucai)*
2 fresh red chillies
1 lime
1 cup bean-sprouts
2 pieces firm white bean curd
2 tablespoons preserved soy beans *(tow cheong)*
1 hard-boiled egg
10 ounces (300 g) medium-sized prawns
1 bundle (about 8 ounces or 225g) rice vermicelli
½ cup oil
2 cloves garlic, chopped
1 tablespoon sugar
1 teaspoon salt
1 tablespoon soy sauce

Soak dried chillies to soften, then pound with 5 shallots. Slice the remaining shallots. Cut chives into 2 inch (5 cm) lengths and shred red chillies. Cut lime into wedges. Remove brown tails of bean-sprouts. Cut bean curd pieces into 1 inch (2½ cm) by ¼ inch (½ cm) pieces. Pound the preserved soy beans to a paste. Slice the hard-boiled egg. Shell, devein and dice the prawns. Soak rice vermicelli in water to soften.

Heat 4 tablespoons oil and fry bean curd slices till firm and lightly browned. Remove and drain well. Brown sliced shallots and keep them for garnishing. Brown garlic and fry the soy bean paste for 1 minute, then add 1 cup water and 1 tablespoon sugar to it and let it simmer gently for 5-10 minutes to get a well flavoured gravy. Season to taste and serve it in a sauceboat.

Heat 4 tablespoons oil and fry the pounded chillies and shallots for 1 minute. Add prawns, half of the fried bean curd and ½ teaspoon salt. Cook for 3-4 minutes till prawns are done. Dish up about half of this mixture for garnishing.

Add soaked rice vermicelli to the remaining mixture in the pan and toss together until well mixed. Add bean-sprouts, chives and about 1 tablespoon soy sauce. Toss together for another 2 minutes, season well and serve it neatly. Spread extra prawn mixture on top and garnish with browned shallots, shredded chillies and sliced egg. Serve lime wedges and gravy separately.

Desserts and Snacks

Serikaya (Egg Custard)

Preparation: 40-50 mins.
Cooking   : 3-4 hrs.

1 cup eggs
2 cups sugar
1 cup thick coconut milk
3 *pandan* **leaves**

The cup of coconut milk should be extracted without adding any water to grated coconut. You may need about 1½ coconuts for this purpose.

Beat the eggs and sugar in a heat-proof container till sugar dissolves. Add coconut milk and mix well. The container holding the custard must not be allowed to come into direct contact with heat, so place it on a metal stand in a much larger pot of boiling water to steam. Steam uncovered for 1 hour, stirring continuously. After that, cover both containers and allow the custard to steam over vigorously boiling water for 2 hours. Add more boiling water to the larger pot every ½ hour and at the same time stir the custard well.

After 3 hours' steaming, the mixture should be golden brown. Add *pandan* leaves and allow it to finish steaming for another hour without stirring. Cool before filling into clean, warm bottles.

Note: Water must never be allowed to drip into the Serikaya. To prevent condensation from the under surface of the lid of the Seri-kaya container, fold an absorbent cloth like muslin a few times so that it is thick but still larger than the lid and place this cloth over the container before putting the lid on. The cloth will absorb condensing steam. When cooling the custard after steaming, remove the lid.

Pulut Tai-Tai

10 ounces (300 g.) glutinous rice
½ coconut, grated
24 to 30 Clitoria flowers
blue colouring
¼ teaspoon salt
2 *pandan* **leaves**
a piece of banana leaf, greaseproof paper *or*
   tin foil

Wash and soak rice for at least 3 hours.
Extract first and second coconut milk from the grated coconut. Wash and pound the clitoria flowers and extract the juice. Add 1 teaspoon of water to the flowers and try to get more juice, if less than 1 teaspoonful juice is obtained. If water has to be added, add 2 to 3 drops of colouring to help deepen the colour.

Drain the rice and put it into the prepared steaming tray with the second coconut milk and the *pandan* leaves. Steam the rice over boiling water for 20 minutes. Then remove the rice from the steamer and add in the first milk and salt. With a fork or a pair of chop-sticks, mix the rice and coconut milk well to-gether. Colour about ⅓ of the rice blue with the colouring the return the rice to steam for another 10 minutes.

Remove the rice from the steamer when it is well cooked. Spoon the rice into a loaf tin that has been rinsed with water, alternating the blue with the white rice.
With a piece of folded banana leaf or grease-proof paper, level off the top and press the rice down as much as possible. Cover the top with the piece of banana leaf, greaseproof paper or tin foil and place something very heavy on top to weigh down the rice.

When the rice is cooled, cut into slices and serve it with *Serikaya.*

From left to right — Kuih Kosui (top left), Kuih Talam,
Kuih Bengka Ubi, Kuih Bengka, Kuih Lapis

Recipe: pp. 115, 107, 108

Serikaya (top)
Pulut Tai Tai (bottom)

Recipe p. 98

100

Cendol

Recipe: p. 103

Agar-Agar Ubi Santan

Recipe: p. 105

Bubur Cha-Cha

Preparation : 30 mins.
Cooking   : 25 mins.

10 ounces (300 g) sweet potato
10 ounces (300 g) yam
½ coconut, grated
8 ounces (225 g) sugar
pinch of salt
2 *pandan* leaves

Peel and dice sweet potato and yam into ½ inch (1 cm) cubes. Steam the cubes for about 15 minutes when it should be cooked.

Without adding water to the grated coconut, extract ½ cup coconut milk. Then add some water and extract 3 cups coconut milk.

Place the second extraction of coconut milk, sugar, salt and *pandan* leaves in a saucepan

and bring to a boil, then add the cooked yam and sweet potato. When the coconut milk boils again, add the first extraction of coconut milk. Remove the saucepan from heat as soon as the milk comes to a boil again.

Serve Bubur Cha-Cha hot or cold. If serving it cold, reduce the second extraction of coconut milk to 2 cups, chill cooked Bubur Cha-Cha and serve with crushed ice.

Cendol

Preparation : 30 mins.
Cooking   : 25 mins.

10 *pandan* leaves
a few drops of green food colouring
½ cup green pea flour
5 tablespoons palm sugar
1 tablespoon sugar
1 coconut, grated
pinch of salt

Pound *pandan* leaves or use an electric blender to extract *pandan* juice. Add sufficient water to *pandan* juice with green food colouring to make 2 cups. Mix green pea flour with the 2 cups of *pandan* juice. Cook this mixture over medium heat stirring continuously till it bubbles.

Place a cendol frame over a basin of cold water which contains some ice cubes. Spoon the cooked mixture on to the cendol frame and with a spatula press it through the holes

into the cold water. Drain off the water and chill the cendol.

Boil the palm sugar and white sugar with ½ cup water to get a syrup. Strain and cool the syrup.

Add 2 cups water to the grated coconut and extract coconut milk. Add a good pinch of salt to the milk.

To serve, place 1 tablespoon cendol into a small serving bowl, then add 1 tablespoon syrup and ¼ cup coconut milk. Top the bowl with ice shavings and serve at once.

Note: If pure green pea flour is used, mix 2½ cups of *pandan* juice to ½ cup green pea flour.

Coconut Cream

Preparation : 50-60 mins.

½ cup evaporated milk
3 teaspoons gelatine
½ cup warm water
½ coconut, grated
6 tablespoons sugar
1 tablespoon desiccated coconut
2-3 glace cherries

Chill evaporated milk. Dissolve the gelatine in ½ cup warm water. Add a little boiled and cooled water and extract 1 cup coconut milk. Add sugar to coconut milk in a large mixing bowl standing in a basin of ice. When sugar is dissolved, add dissolved gelatine to the coconut milk and stir the mixture till it begins to thicken.

Add cold milk to this mixture and whisk it briskly till it resembles whipped cream. Pour the mixture into a rinsed serving bowl and chill in the refrigerator till it sets.

Just before serving, sprinkle desiccated coconut on top and decorate with halved cherries.

Kuih Jagung

Preparation : 20 mins.
Cooking   : 8-10 mins.

½ coconut, grated
½ packet (50 g) green pea flour
¾ cup sugar
pinch of salt
2 *pandan* leaves
1 cup creamed corn
colouring

Extract 2½ cups coconut milk from the grated coconut.

Blend flour, sugar, salt and coconut milk together in a pan, making sure that there are no lumps of flour. Add *pandan* leaves or a few drops of vanilla essence and cook the mixture over a medium fire, stirring all the time till it bubbles. Add creamed corn and colouring, stir for a minute, then pour into 4 rinsed sundae glasses. Chill well before serving.

Note:
1 The mixture can be set in a tray and cut into pieces before serving.

2 Make boats or baskets with banana leaves which have been softened by scalding and set the mixture in them, if preferred.

104

Agar-Agar Gula Goreng

Preparation : 5 mins.
Cooking   : 20-25 mins.

⅓ ounce (10 g) agar-agar strands *or* 6 teaspoons
    agar-agar powder
7 tablespoons sugar
2 egg yolks
⅓ cup evaporated milk
2¼ cups water
1 cup granulated sugar
8 tablespoons water

Combine agar-agar strands or powder and 2¼ cups cool water and boil to dissolve the agar-agar. Add 7 tablespoons sugar and boil till sugar dissolves. Strain the liquid. Beat egg yolks with evaporated milk and stir this into the agar-agar mixture.

To make the caramel, put granulated sugar and water in a heavy pan and cook over very low heat. Stir constantly and do not allow the solution to come to a boil till all the sugar has melted. When this happens, increase the heat, stop stirring and allow it to boil till it is a deep golden colour.

Stir the agar-agar mixture into the caramel over medium heat. When the caramel and agar-agar are thoroughly mixed, pour into a rinsed mould and chill to set.

When the agar-agar has set, turn it out and serve with mixed fruit.

Agar-Agar Ubi Santan

Preparation : 30 mins.
Cooking   : 20 mins.

6 ounces (150 g) sweet potato (white variety)
½ ounce (15 g) agar-agar strands *or* 8 teaspoons
    agar-agar powder
3 cups cool water
2 *pandan* leaves
¾ cup sugar
yellow colouring
½ coconut, grated
2 teaspoons cocoa

Scrub and boil the sweet potato. When it is cooked, skin and mash it by passing through a sieve to remove all the fibres.

Add agar-agar strands or powder to 3 cups cool water in a pan and boil with *pandan* leaves till agar-agar dissolves. Add sugar, stir to dissolve the sugar, then strain the liquid.

Mix a little less than half the agar-agar with mashed potato, add a few drops of yellow colouring, and pour it into a rinsed mould. Chill to set.

Without adding water to the grated coconut, extract coconut milk. This should be done quickly and be ready while the remaining agar-agar is still hot. Stir the milk into the remaining agar-agar and keep it warm so that it does not set.

When the yellow layer of agar-agar has set, scratch its surface with a fork and pour a ½ inch (1 cm) layer of white agar-agar on top of it. Chill to set the second layer.

In the meantime, blend cocoa with 1 tablespoon water. Add the blended cocoa to the rest of the agar-agar and boil it to cook the cocoa. When the white layer has set, scratch its surface and pour brown agar-agar over it. Chill once again to set then turn out to serve.

Pineapple Jam

Preparation: 30 mins.
Cooking   : 1 hr.

4 not-too-ripe pineapples
3 inch (7⅔ cm) stick cinnamon
6 cloves
sugar

Skin pineapple and remove the eyes. Grate them in a circular motion so that there is not too much fibre. Leave the grated pineapple in a sieve for 10 minutes for pineapple juice to drain off. (Cool the juice in the refrigerator — it makes a refreshing drink.)

Measure grated pineapple pulp. For every 1½ cups pulp, use 1 cup sugar. Place pineapple pulp, cinnamon and cloves in a saucepan and allow to boil for about ½ hour to reduce water content. Boil over medium fire and stir frequently to prevent burning. When the pineapple looks dry, add the measured amount of sugar and cook very slowly, stirring all the while, until the jam is a golden colour and of the desired consistency. This takes from ½ hour to 1 hour.

Pour jam into warmed jars and cover immediately.

Pineapple Tarts

Preparation: 1½ hrs.
Cooking   : 30 mins.
Makes   : 60

2 cups flour
10 tablespoons margarine
1 egg yolk
1 egg white
2 tablespoons cold water
½ teaspoon salt
1 cup pineapple jam

Sieve flour and salt together into a bowl. Cut margarine into flour till it is in small pieces. Using fingertips, rub margarine quickly into the flour until there are no big lumps. Beat yolk with cold water and add it to the flour. Mix till pastry binds together. If necessary, add a little more cold water.

Sprinkle a little flour on a clean, smooth table-top or a pastry-board. Dip a tart cutter of about 1 inch (2½ cm) diameter in the flour. Working with a large handful of pastry at a time, knead lightly on the working surface and roll out to ¼ inch (½ cm) thickness. With the floured tart cutter, cut out the rounds as closely as possible. Make a very slight depression of about ½ inch (1¼ cm) diameter in the centre of each round of pastry. Fill this with pineapple jam. Decorate the edge with pastry pincers.

Roll a piece of left-over pastry until it is as thin as can be handled. With a pastry roller, cut thin strips to decorate the tarts.

Brush the tarts with beaten egg white and bake in a moderately hot oven (375°F or 190°C) for 25-30 minutes or till pastry is cooked and evenly browned. Cool tarts on a wire tray before storing.

Kuih Bengka

Preparation: 25 mins.
Cooking   : 1 hr.

1 coconut, grated
¾ cup damp rice flour
2 tablespoons green pea flour
1 cup sugar
⅛ teaspoon salt
1 banana leaf

Without adding water to the grated coconut, extract thick coconut milk. Then add water and extract another 2 cups coconut milk.

Knead rice flour, green pea flour and sugar with the first extraction of coconut milk till sugar is dissolved. Add salt and enough liquid from the second extraction of coconut milk to get 3⅓ cups batter.

Strain batter through a fine hairsieve into a large saucepan. Cook batter, stirring all the time with a wooden spoon until it thickens and bubbles.

Pour cooked custard into an 8 inch (20 cm) square tin lined with softened banana leaves, level off the top and bake in a hot oven (400°F or 200°C) for 1 hour when the top and sides should be well browned.

Cool Kuih Bengka thoroughly before cutting into ½ inch (1 cm) slices for serving.

Note: To soften banana leaves, hold them over a flame for a minute or until they change colour.

Kuih Bengka Ubi

Preparation: 35-40 mins.
Cooking   : 1½ hours

¾ coconut, grated
1 pound (450 g) tapioca
1 tablespoon tapioca flour
6 ounces (180 g) sugar
5 tablespoons palm sugar
pinch of salt

Without adding water to the coconut, extract ½ cup coconut milk. Then add a little water and extract another ½ cup coconut milk. Let coconut milk stand for ½ hour in the refrigerator and then skim off the top.

Grate the tapioca. Mix grated tapioca, tapioca flour, sugar, palm sugar, salt and 1 cup coconut milk (obtained by mixing both extractions of coconut milk) together to get a mixture that is fairly liquid in consistency and which does not stick to the palm when pressed against it.

Pour the mixture into a well greased, 8 inch (20 cm) square tray and bake in a moderate oven (375°F or 190°C) for 1-1½ hours. Cool thoroughly before cutting into ½ inch (1 cm) slices.

Kuih Lapis

Preparation: 30 mins.
Cooking   : 30 mins.

½ coconut, grated
¾ cup damp rice flour
1 tablespoon tapioca flour
1 tablespoon cornflour
1 cup granulated sugar
red and yellow food colouring

Without adding water to the grated coconut, extract thick coconut milk. Then add water and extract 1 ½ cups coconut milk.

Knead both kinds of flour with sugar and the first extraction of coconut milk until sugar dissolves. Mix in enough liquid from the second extraction of coconut milk to get 3 cups batter. Strain batter through muslin and divide it into two equal parts. Colour one part pink by adding a few drops of red food colouring.

Heat an 8 inch (20 cm) steaming tray and steam a thin layer of pink batter for 5 minutes till it is cooked. Ladle a thin layer of white batter on top of the pink and steam it for 3 minutes. Continue steaming thin layers, alternating the pink with the white and making sure each layer is cooked before adding the next layer.

When just enough batter for one layer remains, colour it bright red by adding a little more red colouring and a little yellow colouring to it before spreading it over the steamed kuih.

Note: Make sure the steaming tray is absolutely level before ladling on the batter. If it slopes even slightly, the layers will not be even. Use one ladle for each colour and do not mix them or the colours may "run".

Kuih Keria

Preparation: 40 mins.
Cooking   : 25-30 mins.

1⅓ pounds (600 g) sweet potatoes
2 ounces (60 g) flour
2 ounces (60 g) tapioca flour
4 ounces (120 g) granulated sugar
3 tablespoons water
oil for deep-fat frying

Scrub sweet potatoes and boil them in their jackets. When sweet potatoes are cooked, peel and mash them. Pass mashed potato through a sieve to remove all fibres. Mix in flour and knead together to get a firm dough. If sweet potatoes are very dry, add a little water to make dough more manageable.

Turn dough onto a floured board and roll it into a long roll of 2 inch (5 cm) diameter. Cut the roll into 12 equal slices. Shape each slice into a round cake of ½ inch (1 cm) thickness. With the handle of a wooden spoon, make a hole in the centre of each cake. Fry sweet potato rings in hot oil till they are golden brown. Drain them and keep aside.

Strain the oil left in the frying pan and put sugar and 3 tablespoons water into it. Melt sugar and boil until a very thick syrup is obtained. The thick syrup should be covered with white, close bubbles when it is ready. Return cakes to the pan and toss them in syrup until they are well coated and sugar crystallizes. Serve neatly.

Note: Kuih Keria is also known as potato doughnut.

Kuih Rose

Preparation: 15 mins.
Cooking   : 30 mins.
Makes   : 24

¼ coconut
¾ cup flour
4 tablespoons rice flour
3 tablespoons sugar
1 egg
oil for deep-fat frying

Extract 1 cup coconut milk. Sieve both kinds of flour into a bowl, add sugar and mix well. Make a well in the centre, drop in the egg and half the coconut milk and mix to get a smooth batter. Add the remaining coconut milk, beat the batter for 10 minutes and then let it rest for ½ hour.

Heat the oil for deep-fat frying and heat the kueh rose mould in oil.

When both oil and mould are hot, lift the mould, shake away excess oil and dip it into the batter so that the batter nearly reaches the top of the mould. The mould should be evenly coated with a thin layer of batter. Hold the mould in hot oil and shake it gently when the batter browns and hardens so that it comes away from the mould. Fry Kuih Rose until they are golden brown. Drain well and cool before storing in an airtight tin.

Curry Puffs

Preparation: 50-60 mins.
Cooking   : 10-15 mins.

Pastry
1½ cups flour
5 tablespoons margarine
¼ teaspoon salt

Filling
3 ounces (75 g) lean meat, any kind
1 potato
2 shallots
1 level tablespoon curry powder
4 curry leaves
oil for deep-fat frying

Mince the meat. Dice potato and chop shallots. Mix curry powder with a little water to get a paste.

Heat 2 tablespoons oil and brown chopped shallots. Add curry leaves and curry paste and fry for 2-3 minutes. Add meat and fry for another 2-3 minutes. Add potato, salt and ½ cup water. Cover and cook until potato is soft and filling dry, about 15-20 minutes. Season and cool the filling thoroughly.

Sieve flour into a bowl. Cut margarine into flour until it is in small pieces. With fingertips, rub margarine into flour very quickly until dough is evenly mixed. Add enough cold water, about 3 tablespoons, to bind pastry. Turn the pastry onto a floured board and roll it out to ⅒ inch (¼ cm) thickness. Cut it into rounds with a 2 inch (5 cm) cutter.

Put an equal amount of filling on each round of pastry, wet the edges of pastry rounds and fold over to make curry puffs. Press the edges together and twist the edge to seal.

Fry curry puffs slowly in lightly smoking oil till pastry is thoroughly cooked. Drain well and serve.

Put an equal amount of filling on each round of pastry, wet the edges of pastry rounds and fold over to make curry puffs. Press the edges together and twist the edge to seal.

Kuih Kochi

Preparation: 30-35 mins.
Cooking   : 20-25 mins.

10 pieces banana leaves
¾ cup damp glutinous rice (*pulut*) flour
1 tablespoon sugar
2½ tablespoons *pandan* juice

Filling
¼ coconut, grated
4 tablespoons palm sugar
1 tablespoon sugar
1 teaspoon tapioca flour

Scald the banana leaf to soften, then fold into cones about 4 inches (10 cm) deep. Grease them well.

Make the filling. Dissolve palm sugar and 1 tablespoon white sugar in 2 tablespoons water. Add grated coconut and cook till coconut is soft and dry. Blend tapioca flour with 2 teaspoons water and add to coconut to bind it. Cool the filling and shape into 10 even-sized balls.

Knead damp glutinous rice flour with 1 tablespoon sugar and *pandan* juice to get a soft tacky dough. Divide dough into 10 portions.

Divide each portion of dough into 2 unequal halves. Take the bigger half and press it into the tip of the cone and up the sides. Put a portion of the filling into the hollow and cover with the smaller piece of dough. Fold cone over to get a good shape and a firm base. Steam the cones for 20 minutes over boiling water.

If the Kuih Kochi lose their shape during steaming, refold after cooking.

Note: Kuih Kochi can be plain white or blue in colour. Two-coloured Kuih Kochi—white and green or white and blue—are very attractive.

Banana Pancakes

Preparation: 15 mins.
Cooking   : 20-30 mins.

1 cup flour
1 teaspoon baking power
2 eggs
½ cup milk
6 large ripe bananas (*pisang rajah*)
1½ tablespoons castor sugar
pinch of salt
1 tablespoon oil
2 tablespoons sugar
1 lemon

Sieve flour and baking powder into a bowl. Make a well in the centre, add the eggs and half of the milk, mix well, and beat batter for 10 minutes till it is smooth and light. Add the reamining milk.

Mash bananas together with castor sugar and salt. Mix mashed bananas with the batter.

Grease a frying pan, heat it and fry pancakes till they are brown on both sides. Grease the pan after each pancake has been removed.

Turn pancakes out onto sugared paper, sprinkle each with a little sugar and a squeeze of lemon juice. Fold into quarters and serve hot.

Lontong

Recipe: p. 7

Roti Jala

Recipe: p. 127

112

Otak Otak

Recipe: p. 49

Rampa Udang

Recipe: p. 119

Kuih Kosui

Preparation: 25 mins.
Cooking   : 20 mins.

1 cup sugar (8 tablespoons chopped palm
    sugar, the remainder granulated sugar)
½ cup damp rice flour
4 tablespoons tapioca flour
1 teaspoon alkali water
⅓ coconut (grated fine and white)
pinch of salt

Dissolve sugar in 1 cup boiling water and cool the syrup.

Knead damp rice flour and tapioca flour together, then knead in the cool syrup. Stir in enough water to get 3 cups batter. Add alkali water and strain batter through muslin.

Heat an 8 inch (20 cm) steaming tray, pour in batter, stirring all the while till it begins tc thicken. Cover it and steam for 20 minutes.

Mix grated coconut with salt. When the kuih is cool, cut it up neatly with a knife dipped in cold water and toss each piece in the coconut so that it is coated all over. Serve neatly.

Note: For green Kuih Kosui, leave out the palm sugar and add *pandan* juice with a few drops of green food colouring. When this batter is cooked in small Chinese wine cups, it is known as *Kuih Lompang*.

Kuih Talam

Preparation: 45 mins.
Cooking   : 40-50 mins.

Green layer
½ cup damp rice flour
4 tablespoons tapioca flour
1 tablespoon green pea flour
¾ cup sugar
12 pandan leaves
few drops green food colouring
1 teaspoon alkali water *(kan sui)*

White layer
4 tablespoons damp rice flour
1 tablespoon green pea flour
1 coconut, grated
¼ teaspoon salt

Dissolve sugar in 1 cup water to obtain syrup. Cool the syrup. Extract *pandan* juice from *pandan* leaves.

For the green layer — knead the rice, tapioca and green pea flours together. Knead in syrup and enough water to get 3 cups batter. Add alkali water and green colouring before straining through a piece of thin muslin.

For the white layer — extract 1 cup santan. Mix rice flour and green pea flour with the santan to get 1½ cups batter. Add salt and strain through a piece of thin muslin. Test-steam batters for consistency. In a small enamel plate, steam 2 tablespoons of the green batter for 10 minutes. This thin layer of batter should be very soft and jelly-like. Test-steam the white layer — it should be soft and barely able to hold itself up when cooked.

Heat an 8-inch steaming tray. Pour in green batter and stir over medium heat till batter begins to thicken and flecks can be seen floating in the batter. Cover the steam for 20 minutes, when the top should be bubbly.

Use a clean piece of damp, thin muslin to blot any remaining liquid from the surface of this green layer before gently pouring the white batter onto it. Cover and steam for 10 minutes over medium heat. When cooked, the white layer should be set but not wrinkled. Cool thoroughly before cutting.

Note: 1. For a brown and white Kuih Talam, omit the pandan juice. Chop up ½ piece *gula melaka* and mix it with enough granulated sugar to make ¾ cups.
   2. Test-steaming for consistency is very essential as the liquid content of damp rice flour varies greatly. If batters are found to be too thick, resulting in thin layers on the plate that can be peeled off, add more water or santan to the batter and test-steam again.

115

Ondeh-Ondeh

Preparation: 40 mins.
Cooking   : 15-20 mins.

pandan **juice from 10 leaves**
¼ coconut, grated white
4 tablespoons palm sugar
3 teaspoons granulated sugar ·
½ cup damp glutinous rice *(pulut)* **flour**
pinch of salt

To obtain *pandan* juice from the leaves, you have to pound the leaves very finely, then strain. To prepare white grated coconut, use a sharp knife to peel off the dark-brown skin of the white kernel before grating. Chop palm sugar and mix it with the white sugar.

Mix damp glutinous rice flour with *pandan* juice to get a stiff dough. Take a piece of dough the size of a marble, press it into a flat disc and cook it in a saucepan of boiling water. When it boils and floats, take it out, drain it and knead it into the uncooked dough to get a smooth and pliable dough.

Roll the dough into a long roll of 1 inch (2½ cm) diameter and cut it into pieces the size of small marbles. With fingers, shape each piece into a cup and put some of the mixed sugar in the hollow. Draw dough together to close the mouth and shape into a round ball.

Cook balls of dough in quickly boiling water until they float. Drain them well and toss them in grated coconut mixed with a pinch of salt.

Serve ondeh-ondeh in banana leaf "baskets".

Ondeh-Ondeh Keledek

Preparation: 1 hour
Cooking   : 6-8 mins.

4 tablespoons palm sugar
2 teaspoons sugar
¼ coconut, grated white
pinch of salt
1½ tablespoons flour
1 tablespoon tapioca flour
10 ounces (300 g) sweet potatoes (the ones with
    white centres)
1½ tablespoons *pandan* **juice**
a few drops of green food colouring

Chop the palm sugar and mix it with white sugar. Remove the dark skin from the white coconut kernel before grating. Mix grated coconut with a pinch of salt. Sieve both kinds of flour.

Clean and boil sweet potatoes in their jackets till cooked. When cool, skin and mash them and mix with both kinds of flour to get a pliable dough. Add *pandan* juice to get a good green colour and flavour.

Roll dough out into a long thin roll of about 1 inch (2½ cm) diameter and cut it into pieces the size of small marbles. Shape each piece into a cup and put some of the sugar mixture into the hollow. Draw the dough together to close and shape into a neat ball.

Cook balls of dough in boiling water until they float. Drain well and toss them in grated coconut. Serve ondeh-ondeh keledek in banana-leaf boats.

116

Sago Pudding

Preparation : 40 mins.
Cooking   : 5-8 mins.

1½ cups sago
1 egg white
2 tablespoons brandy
5 tablespoons chopped palm sugar
2 tablespoons sugar
1 coconut, grated
pinch of salt

Wash and soak sago for 30 minutes. Drain sago and put in a large sieve. Pour boiling water over the sago until it looks transparent. Shake the sieve to remove water.

Whisk egg white with the brandy in it. Mix whisked egg white into sago and turn the mixture into a rinsed mould. Chill the sago.

Put palm sugar into a saucepan with sugar and 1 cup water to boil. Reduce the syrup to about 1 cup and strain it into a small jug. Cool to room temperature before serving.

Add a little boiled water to the grated coconut and extract 1 cup coconut milk. Add a pinch of salt to the milk and serve it in a jug.

When sago is well chilled, turn it out and serve with syrup and coconut milk.

Yam Cake

Preparation: 40 mins.
Cooking   : 40 mins.

2 tablespoons fried peanuts
½ tablespoon gingelly seeds
10 ounces (300 g) yam
1 Chinese sausage
1 slice preserved Chinese radish (lopak)
3 stalks spring onions
1 tablespoon dried prawns
2 shallots
5 tablespoons oil
½ cup minced pork
2 teaspoons salt
¼ teaspoon pepper
¼ teaspoon mixed spice (ng heong fun)
4 tablespoons tapioca flour
½ cup damp rice flour
1 teaspoon alkali water

Pound the fried peanuts. Roast gingelly seeds by stir-frying them in a dry pan over low heat till brown. Dice yam into ½ inch (1 cm) cubes, chop sausage, preserved *lopak* and spring onions. Soak chopped preserved *lopak* in water for about ½ hour to remove excess salt. Pound dried prawns and slice shallots.

Heat the oil in a pan and brown shallots. When shallots are lightly browned, add pork, dried prawns, sausage, preserved *lopak* and mushrooms. Stir-fry for a minute. Add yam,

salt, pepper and mixed spice and toss the ingredients well together. When yams are lightly cooked and well coated with oil and other ingredients, dish up and keep aside.

Knead tapioca flour with damp rice flour and mix in enough water to get 2½ cups batter. Add the fried ingredients and alkali water and mix well. Season to taste.

Heat an 8 inch (20 cm) steaming tray, pour in the batter mixture and stir it till it begins to thicken. Allow the mixture to steam for ½ hour.

Remove the yam cake from the steamer, sprinkle spring onions, peanuts and gingelly seeds on top. Cool thoroughly before cutting into neat pieces.

Serve yam cake with chilli sauce.

Note: Cold left-over yam cake can be sliced into ½ inch (1 cm) pieces and fried in a lightly greased pan till brown on both sides. Delicious if served hot with chilli sauce.

Yam Puffs

Preparation: 1 hr.
Cooking   : 15 mins.
Makes   : 12

Pastry
10 ounces (300 g) yam (with head)
1 ounce (30 g) flour
1 ounce (30 g) lard
¼ teaspoon baking powder
¼ teaspoon ammonia bicarbonate
½ teaspoon monosodium glutamate
½ teaspoon sesame oil
pinch of pepper
1 teaspoon sugar
½ teaspoon salt

Filling
7 ounces (200 g) prawns
6 ounces (160 g) pork
3 ounces (80 g) roast pork *(char siew)*
1 teaspoon cornflour
½ egg, beaten
½ teaspoon sesame oil
pinch of pepper
1 teaspoon sugar
½ teaspoon salt
oil for deep-fat frying

To make the pastry dough, slice yam thinly and steam till soft. Mash till fine while still warm. Add all other ingredients listed under "Pastry" and knead till dough is smooth. Keep dough covered till required.

Shell prawns and wash them in salt water. Dice prawns, pork and roast pork.

Heat 1 tablespoon oil and fry pork till it changes colour. Add sesame oil, pepper, sugar and salt, and finally add prawns and roast pork. Add ¼ cup water and fry till filling is cooked and water is absorbed. Blend cornflour with 1 teaspoon water and add it to the filling. Remove pan from fire, pour beaten egg over the ingredients and stir quickly to mix and cook the egg. Cool filling on a plate.

Divide the pastry and filling into 12 portions. Wrap 1 portion of filling in each piece of pastry and shape into a neat puff. Dust fingers with flour if necessary while working.

Fry yam puffs in hot oil over a medium fire till they are brown and puffed up. Drain well and serve.

Jemput Pisang

Preparation: 10 mins.
Cooking   : 10-15 mins.

10 ounces (300 g) bananas *(pisang mas)*
1½ tablespoons sugar
3 heaped tablespoons flour
oil for deep-fat frying

Mash bananas and mix thoroughly with sugar and flour. The dough should have a dropping consistency.

Heat the oil for deep-fat frying. When it is smoking hot, drop in a tablespoon of the mixture at a time into hot oil and fry over medium heat till the banana cakes float and are a dark-brown colour. Try two or three first. If they are too soft for your taste, add a little more dough,

Drain well before serving.

Note: For best results, use really ripe bananas. If bananas are very sweet, use less sugar.

Rampa Udang

Preparation: 1½ hours
Cooking   : 50 mins

¾ coconut, grated
1 piece *cekor*
5 shallots
1 clove garlic
3 candlenuts
6 peppercorns
1 tablespoon coriander
½ cup shelled prawns
2 tablespoons oil
2 teaspoons salt
½ teaspoon sugar
10 ounces (300 g) glutinous rice *(pulut)*
2 *pandan* leaves
12 squares banana leaf of 6 inch (15 cm) width

In a dry pan, fry half the grated coconut until evenly browned. Grind browned coconut till fine.

Grind *cekor,* shallots, garlic, candlenuts, peppercorns and coriander till fine. Coriander grinds easily if roasted first. Dice the prawns.

Heat 2 tablespoons oil and fry ground spices for 3-4 minutes. Add prawns, ½ teaspoon salt and ½ teaspoon sugar and fry till prawns are well cooked. Finally, add ground coconut and mix well. Season to taste and set aside to cool.

Drain glutinous rice which should have been soaked for at least 4 hours. Put it with ½ teaspoon salt and *pandan* leaves, shredded lengthwise and tied into a knot, in a steaming tray and steam for 15 minutes.

Extract ¼ cup coconut milk from the remaining grated coconut. After rice has been steamed for 15 minutes, turn it out into the coconut milk, mix well, and return rice to the steaming tray to steam for another 10 minutes till well cooked.

Scald the pieces of banana leaf to soften. Divide rice and filling into 12 equal portions each. Spread one portion of rice lengthwise in the centre of one banana leaf square. Put filling on it and fold the rice over to shape it into a roll of about 2 inches (5 cm) long and 1 inch (2½ cm) in diameter. Wrap each roll firmly in a piece of banana leaf, press the ends together and staple to secure. Trim away excess lengths of leaf and place wrapped rolls into a hot frying pan to brown leaves all over. Turn rolls to get them evenly browned.

Vadai

Preparation: 30 mins.
Cooking   : 20 mins.

10 ounces (300 g) split black peas
1 onion
3 green chillies
2 sprigs curry leaves
1 teaspoon salt
shake of pepper
banana leaf, about 4 inch (10 cm) square
oil

Wash and soak split peas for at least 4 hours, then grind or blend to a paste inan electric blender.

Dice the onion and chillies very finely. Shred the curry leaves very thinly.

Mix all the ingredients together with salt and

pepper to taste. The mixture should be as soft as one can handle. Spread the banana leaf on a working surface. Brush it with oil. Place a tablespoonful of the mixture on the oily leaf and shape it into a ring. With a quick twist of the wrist turn the leaf over so that the ring slips gently from the oily leaf into a pan of hot oil. Fry till brown and well cooked. Drain well before serving.

Note: Any smooth, flat and oiled surface can take the place of the oiled banana leaf. If desired, a few unshelled shrimps can be pressed into the surface of each ring for added flavour.

119

Shanghai Pancakes

Preparation: 40-50 mins.
Cooking   : 25-30 mins.

10 ounces (300 g) red peas
4-6 ounces (120-180g) sugar
4 tablespoons oil

Batter
1 cup flour
1 egg
1 cup water
pinch of salt
3 tablespoons oil

Paste

Soak 10 ounces (300 g) red peas overnight. Boil them in a pressure cooker for ½ hour. Mash soft peas and pass them through a sieve to remove the tough skin. Pour this puree into a calico bag and hang it up to enable water to drip away. Turn out pea paste onto a frying pan and cook it over low heat with 4-6 ounces (120-180 g) sugar and 4 tablespoons oil. Keep stirring the paste to prevent burning. When paste is ready, it should be very smooth and glossy. This paste can be made beforehand and kept in a refrigerator for up to 10 days.

Batter

Sieve flour and salt into a bowl. Make a well in the centre, put the egg and ½ cup water in the well and mix to get a smooth batter. Beat batter for 10 minutes and then add the rest of the water. Let the batter stand for ½ hour.

Fry pancakes in a hot, greased pan till they are lightly browned on both sides. Turn pancakes out onto a plate, spread pea paste on it and fold the top and bottom over to get a long, rectangular shaped cake that completely covers the pea paste.

When all the pancakes have been filled and folded over, heat 2 tablespoons oil in a frying pan and fry each pancake again till it is well browned. Cut each pancake into 1 inch (2½ cm) pieces and serve sprinkled with sesame seeds.

Note: This pancake is sometimes served with peanut cream.

Peanut Cream

½ cup peanuts
1 tablespoon gingelly seeds
3½ cups water
3 oz sugar
1 tablespoon cornflour (rounded)
¼ cup evaporated milk

Fry peanuts in a pan without oil over low heat till they are brown and cooked. Fry gingelly seeds, without oil, over low heat till they are brown.

Skin the peanuts. Place peanuts, gingelly seeds and 1 cup water in a blender and blend at high speed till smooth. Strain the mixture thorough a sieve into a saucepan, adding the rest of the water to help strain the mixture. Boil the mixture over modate heat, add the sugar and when it boils again, thicken the mixture by adding the blended cornflour (blended with 1½ tablespoons water). Remove pan from the fire and mix in the evaporated milk. Serve hot.

Almond Towfoo and Fruit

Preparation: 5 mins.
Cooking   : 15 mins.

¼ ounce (8 g) *agar-agar* strand *or* 4½
   teaspoons *agar-agar* powder
5 cups water
1 cup evaporated milk
½ cup sugar
½ tablespoon almond essence
1 pineapple
3 cups sugar

Add *agar-agar* strands or powder to 2 cups cool water in a pan and boil till it dissolves. Add evaporated milk and ½ cup sugar and boil again till the sugar has dissolved. Stir in almond essence and strain the liquid into a rinsed tray. Chill to set.

Remove the hard core of the pineapple and dice pineapple into 1 inch (2½ cm) cubes. Boil 2 cups water with 6 tablespoons sugar. When it boils, add pineapple cubes and allow them to stew for 5 minutes. Remove from heat, cool and refrigerate.

When Almond Towfoo has set, cut into 1 inch (2½ cm) cubes. Serve the Almond Towfoo and pineapple cubes chilled in pineapple syrup.

Note: Tinned lychees or longans, watermelon balls and tinned fruit cocktail may be used either with, or in place of, the pineapple.

Pulut Inti

Preparation: 20 mins.
Cooking   : 25 mins.

10 ounces (300 g) glutinous rice *(pulut)*
8 pieces banana leaves of 8 inch (20 cm) width
2 *pandan* leaves
½ coconut, grated
¼ teaspoon salt
4 tablespoons palm sugar
1 tablespoon granulated sugar

Wash and soak glutinous rice for at least 4 hours. Soften the banana leaves by scalding. Shred *pandan* leaves lengthwise and tie into a knot.

Extract 1 cup coconut milk from half the grated coconut. Drain soaked glutinous rice and place it in a steaming tray with salt, coconut milk and knotted *pandan* leaves. Steam rice for 20-25 minutes till it is well cooked. Discard the *pandan* leaves.

Melt palm sugar and granulated sugar with 3 tablespoons water and add the rest of the coconut to it. Cook coconut till it is soft and dry. Cool it on a plate.

Spoon 1 tablespoon cooked rice onto each piece of softened banana leaf, place 1 teaspoon cooked coconut on top of it and wrap around it neatly.

121

Miscellaneous Favourites

Poh Piah

Preparation: 1-1½ hours
Cooking   : 40-50 mins
Makes   : 24 rolls

24 poh piah skins

Garnishes

2 eggs
¼ teaspoon salt
shake of pepper
1 pair Chinese sausages
10 cloves garlic, finely chopped
6 tablespoons oil
20 shallots, sliced
2 pieces firm bean curd, shredded
1 cup bean-sprouts
½ cucumber
1 plant lettuce
1 sprig coriander leaves
15 red chillies
½ cup *teem cheong*
good shake of pepper

Filling

10 ounces (300 g) prawns
2 teaspoons salt
½ teaspoon sugar
10 ounces (300 g) pork
2 pounds (900 g) yam beans
10 French beans
2 tablespoons oil
½ cup crabmeat
2 teaspoons soy sauce

First prepare all garnishes
Beat eggs with ¼ teaspoon salt and a good shake of pepper. Heat and lightly grease a frying pan. Make three very thin omelettes. Roll each omelette into a tight roll and shred very finely. Loosen and pile shredded omelette onto small dish.

Fry sausages till evenly browned. Slice them thinly and put them onto another small dish.

Fry chopped garlic in 2 tablespoons oil until evenly browned. Serve browned garlic and oil in a small dish.

Heat another 2 tablespoons oil and brown sliced shallots. Drain browned shallots and serve them in another small dish.

Fry bean curd shreds till firm, drain well and serve in a small dish.

Remove the straggly brown tails and blanch bean-sprouts. Cut cucumber into ⅓ inch (4/5 cm) fingers. Wash and dry lettuce leaves and coriander leaves. Halve each lettuce leaf along the central vein. Arrange the vegetables neatly on a flat dish. Pound chillies to a fine paste and remove this to a small dish.

Next prepare the filling
Clean, dice and season prawns with ½ teaspoon salt and ½ teaspoon sugar. Clean, parboil and shred pork finely. Shred yam beans and French beans.

Toss shredded French beans in 2 tablespoons hot oil to cook them lightly. Set aside. Fry shredded parboiled pork in the same oil till colour changes and pork is cooked, then add soy sauce and prawns. Stir-fry for a minute. Add yam beans and 1½ teaspoons salt and cook together till yam beans are cooked and a little tender. This should take about 15 minutes. Now mix in the French beans, crabmeat then season to taste and keep hot till required.

To serve
The poh piah skins should be piled on a plate and covered with damp muslin to keep them moist. The hot meat filling is placed in a deep dish surrounded by the garnishes attractively arranged in small dishes around it.

To make poh piah, place a skin on a plate, put a piece of lettuce on it and thinly spread chilli sauce and *teem cheong* on the lettuce. Place a little of each garnish on top of the lettuce and finally spread a tablespoon of the hot filling on top of everything. Fold in the sides first, then one of the other edges. Tuck in firmly and roll up. Poh piah should be eaten immediately for the skin becomes soggy after a while.

Satay

Recipe: p. 31

Steamboat

Recipe: p. 129

A Selection of Ingredients for Asian Cooking

1	*Yow char kway*	12	Soaked cuttlefish	23	Fried egg noodles (fine)	33	Thick rice vermicelli	44	Sharksfin
2	Dried soybean cakes	13	Dried cuttlefish	24	Black shrimp paste	34	*Wonton* egg noodles	45	Fine rice vermicelli
3	Small dried soybean cakes	14	Fried egg noodles	25	Rice vermicelli	35	Firm soybean cake	46	Dried radish
4	Chinese sausages	15	Century eggs	26	Sesame oil	36	Soft soybean cake	47	Young corn cobs
5	Salt fish	16	Salted duck's eggs	27	Preserved soy beans	37	Flat rice noodles	48	Tamarind
6	Rice malt sauce	17	Thick yellow noodles		(light variety)	38	Soybean skin *(fu chok)*	49	Dried lily flowers
7	Black soy sauce	18	*Wonton* skin	28	Oyster sauce	39	*Teem chok*	50	Black sweet malt
8	Light soy sauce	19	Quail's eggs	29	Dried egg noodles	40	Plum sauce	51	Dried anchovies
9	Mushroom sauce	20	Dried prawns	30	*Tow-see*	41	Agar strips	52	Dried shrimp paste
10	Fish sauce	21	Dried young anchovies	31	*Hoi sin* sauce	42	Spring roll skin	53	Transparent noodles
11	Chinese rice wine	22	Green pea flour	32	Macaroni	43	Fresh Hokkien mee	54	Dried tamarind skin

Asian Vegetables, Herbs and Fruits

1 Screwpine leaves	17 Tomatoes	32 Cucumber	45 Chinese chives (with
2 Banana flower	18 Bird chillies	33 Carrot	flowers)
3 Pumpkin	19 Yam	34 Cauliflower	46 Young ginger
4 Winter melon	20 Bamboo shoot	35 Mustard green (*kai choy,*	47 Ginger
5 Long bottle gourd	21 Yam bean	Chinese)	48 Small sour starfruit
6 *Pisang mas*	22 Lady's fingers	36 Radish	49 Chinese spinach (*tong hoe*)
7 *Pisang rajah*	23 Capsicum	37 Red & green chillies	50 Water chestnuts
8 *Pisang tandok*	24 Bittergourd	38 Sweet potato leaves	51 Cabbage
9 *Pisang hijau*	25 Vegetable marrow	39 Chinese white cabbage	52 Basil (*Daun selaseh*)
10 *Petai*	26 Pineapple	40 Leek	53 Basil (*Daun kemangi*)
11 Drumsticks	27 Limes (large), local	41 Potatoes	54 Mint leaves
12 Lemon grass	limes (small)	42 *Bunga kantan*	55 Soybean sprouts
13 Tapioca	28 Lemons	43 French beans	56 Beansprouts
14 Onions	29 Angled loofah	44 Chinese mustard greens	57 Spring onion
15 Garlic	30 Green eggplant	(white stalk variety)	58 Galingale
16 Shallots	31 Purple eggplant		

59 Coriander leaves	
60 Curry leaves	
61 Watercress	
62 Celery	
63 Lettuce	
64 *Kiamchye* (salted	
kuakchye)	
65 *Daun kadeok*	
66 Turmeric leaf	
67 Long beans	
68 Chinese chives	
(without flowers)	
69 *Daun kessom*	
70 Mustard green (*kai choy,* local)	
71 Mustard green (*choy sum*)	

Simple Fritter Batter

Preparation: 5 mins.

4 tablespoons flour
2 tablespoons cornflour
½ teaspoon baking powder
5 tablespoons water
½ teaspoon salt
1 teaspoon oil

Mix all dry ingredients together in a bowl and make a well in the centre.

Add ¾ the measured amount of water to dry ingredients and stir quickly to get a thick batter. Add the rest of the water as batter thickens.

Add the oil and mix till batter is smooth. If batter is too thick, add more water. Use straight away to coat any food for frying.

Note: This batter is easy to make and is light and crisp. It is suitable for both sweet and savoury fritters e.g. prawn fritters, banana fritters, sweet potato fritters.

Roti Jala

Preparation: 15 mins.
Cooking   : 20-25 mins.

1 cup flour
1 egg
½ coconut, grated
2 *pandan* leaves
½ teaspoon salt
1 tablespoon oil

Extract 1 cup coconut milk from the grated coconut. Sift flour and salt into a mixing bowl. Make a well in the centre and drop in the egg and half the coconut milk.

With a wooden spoon, stir egg and coconut milk into the flour to get a smooth batter. Add more coconut milk if necessary. Beat the batter for about 10 minutes till it is smooth and bubbly.

Mix the rest of the coconut milk into the batter, cover the bowl with a tea towel and leave the batter to stand for 20 minutes.

Fold *pandan* leaves and tie them together to get a 6 inch (15 cm) brush. If *pandan* leaves are not available, tie a piece of clean muslin to the end of a stick.

Heat a frying pan and grease it by brushing with the *pandan* or muslin brush dipped in oil.

Pour some batter into a roti jala mould and, moving it in a circular motion, let it drop to form a thin, lacy pancake in the hot frying pan. When it is cooked, fold it into quarters and transfer to a plate. Cover with a clean tea towel to keep it moist and warm. Continue making roti jala, one at a time, till all the batter is used up.

To serve, stack roti jala neatly on a plate. Serve chicken curry with it.

Kuih Pietee (Tophats)

Preparation: 20 mins.
Cooking   : 40-50 mins.

4 tablespoons flour
¾ cup rice flour
1 egg
¾ cup coconut milk *or* water
¼ teaspoon salt
oil for deep-fat frying

Sift both kinds of flour and salt into a mixing bowl. Make a well in the centre, add the egg and liquid (coconut milk or water) and mix to get a smooth batter. Beat batter for 10 minutes till it is bubbly. Cover batter and let it rest for 20 minutes.

Heat a saucepan two-thirds full of oil for deep-fat frying. Heat the pietee mould in hot oil.

When the mould is well heated and oil is smoking hot, lift it out and give it a gentle shake to remove excess oil before dipping it batter. The batter should just reach the top of the mould.

Immerse batter-covered mould in hot oil and shake it up and down a couple of times so that batter at the top which is still soft will fall away from the mould, forming the brim of the hat. When the hat is brown, a gentle shake loosens it from the mould. Lift hats up with a perforated spoon and drain them well. Cool and store in airtight containers.

It might take 5-10 spoilt hats before the mould becomes "seasoned", but when this happens and the oil is at the correct temperature, the hats can be made very quickly.

To serve, fill tophats with *Poh Piah* filling (see page 122). Garnish with coriander leaves, a little sprig on top of each hat, and chilli sauce.

Soybean Milk

Preparation: 20 mins.
Cooking   : 10-15 mins.

5 ounces (150 g) soy beans
¾ cup granulated sugar
2 slices ginger
2 *pandan* leaves

Wash and soak beans for at least 4 hours. Put beans with 2 cups water in a blender. Blend at high speed till a smooth pulp is obtained. Pour pulp from blender into a calico bag and squeeze it through 4 cups of water. Squeeze pulp until it is really dry.

Pour soybean milk into a saucepan, add *pandan* leaves and ginger slices to it and bring it to a boil. When it boils, add sugar. As soon as it boils again, remove the pan from heat.

Soybean milk can be served hot or cold. When chilled, it is a very refreshing drink.

Steamboat

Preparation: 1-1½ hours

Serves   : 4-6

8 ounces (225 g) chicken meat
8 ounces (225 g) fillet steak
1 teaspoon soy sauce for marinating
1 teaspoon sesame oil
2 teaspoons cornflour
8 ounces (225 g) pig's liver
8 ounces (225 g) threadfin *(ikan kura)*
1 teaspoon salt
ginger juice from 1 inch (2⅔ cm) piece ginger
8-12 large prawns
1 teaspoon sugar
2 pieces soft white bean curd
8 ounces (225 g) lettuce
8 ounces (225 g) spinach
8 ounces (225 g) Chinese cabbage
4 ounces (120 g) rice vermicelli *or* transparent
    noodles
½ cup chilli sauce
1 tablespoon soy sauce per person (served in
    individual saucers)
½ cup lard
1 egg per person
a large saucepan full of chicken *and/or* pork
    stock

Slice chicken and steak as thinly as possible and marinate steak in 1 teaspoon soy sauce, sesame oil and 1 teaspoon cornflour.

Slice liver and fish to 1/10 inch (¼ cm) thickness and marinate liver in ½ teaspoon salt, 1 teaspoon cornflour and ginger juice.

Clean prawns and remove shell between head and tail. Slit back of prawns and devein them. Season in 1 teaspoon sugar and ½ teaspoon salt.

Cut each piece of bean curd into 4 pieces. Cut lettuce, spinach and cabbage into 2 inch (5 cm) lengths.

Soak rice vermicelli or transparent noodles in water till soft. Drain well and remove to a dish.

Lay each type of vegetable on a flat plate and arrange one type of sliced meat on each bed of vegetables. Prawns, sliced fish and bean curd can be arranged on one plate. Chilli sauce, soy sauce and lard should be ladled out into several small saucers and placed conveniently around the table.

The steamboat pot is placed at the centre with the dishes of vegetable and meat surrounding it. The stock should be boiling in the pot at the start of the meal and should be maintained at a gentle boil throughout, with more stock added from time to time when ever necessary.

Each diner has a small dish and a bowl in front of him. He may beat his egg immediately in the bowl with a teaspoon of soy sauce or leave the egg till the end of the meal. Using a pair of chopsticks or a long wire ladle, each person selects some meat and vegetable and dips it into the section of the pot directly in front of him. When cooking vegetables in the stock he should spoon a little lard over the vegetable. The cooked food may be dipped into the beaten egg to lightly cool it so that it is the right temperature for eating. It can also be dipped in chilli sauce or soy sauce.

The diner who wishes to have some rice vermicelli or transparent noodles to go with the food will put a little rice vermicelli or transparent noodles into his bowl (either over any egg that is left or without the egg) and soup is ladled over the vermicelli/noodles.

Note: Instead of a proper steamboat pot, an electric rice cooker may be used.

Menu Suggestions

Simple daily lunches or dinners (4 to 6 persons)

(serve fresh fruits as dessert)

1. Savoury Rice
   Kerabu Timun
   Beef Soup

2. Rice with Long Beans
   Sambal Blacan
   Fish Ball Soup

3. Salt Fish Rice
   Spinach Masak Lemak
   Sambal Blacan

4. Fried Rice
   Kerabu Pineapple
   Dumpling Soup

5. Chicken Rice in Clay Pot
   Fried Shredded Vegetable Marrow
   Szechuan Vegetable and Pork Soup

6. Steamed Chicken with Sausage
   Pork Balls and Beancurd Soup
   Rice

7. Minced Pork steamed with
   Mushrooms
   Fried Stuffed Hardtail
   Masak Lodeh
   Rice

8. Fried Beef with Spring Onions
   Gulai Tumis
   Loh Hon Chye
   Rice

9. Sambal Prawns
   Scrambled Eggs with Onions
   Braised Vegetable Marrow
   Rice

10. Beef Rendang
    Fried Assam Prawns
    Sambal Ikan Bilis
    Nasi Lemak

11. Chicken Curry
    Egg and Fish Roll
    Fried Diced Long Beans
    Rice

12. Sweet Sour Pork
    Mussels in Tow-cheong
    Eggplant with Crab Sauce

Informal lunches or dinners (6 to 8 persons)

1. Laksa
   Kuih Jagung

2. Mee Siam
   Coconut Cream

3. Har Mee
   Chinese Roast Pork
   Shanghai Pancakes

4. Otak-otak
   Teochew Duck
   Spring Rolls
   Eggplant with Crab Sauce

6. Ayam Golek
   Beef Curry
   Gado-gado
   Masak Lodeh
   Lontong
   Bubur Cha-cha

5. Chicken Curry
   Fried Masak Lemak
   Kerabu Kobis
   Roti Jala
   Agar-agar Ubi Santan

Special occasions (8 to 10 persons)

1. Spring Chicken
   Sweet Sour Spareribs
   Spring Rolls
   Coconut Cream
   Kerabu Pineapple

2. Chicken Curry
   Otak-otak
   Egg and Fish Roll
   Pecal
   Kerabu Kobis
   Roti Jala
   Sago Pudding

3. Duck Stewed with young ginger
   Chinese Roast Pork
   Kwai Fah Chee
   Braised Vegetable Marrow
   Steamed Melon Soup
   Fried Mee-Cantonese style
   Shanghai Pancakes

4. Beef Rendang
   Chicken Kurmah
   Sambal Prawns
   Gado-gado
   Nasi Kunyit
   Cendol

Cocktail (10 to 15 persons)

Five-spiced Chicken
Spring Rolls
Satay
Lontong
Fish Cakes
Kuih Pietee
Kuih Talam
Assorted Drinks

Glossary

AGAR-AGAR
Tai choy koh (C)
大菜糕

A seaweed used widely in Asia for making jellies. It has better setting qualities than gelatine and sets without refrigeration. Available in powder form in packets, or in strands from Chinese grocer stores or health food stores.

ALKALI WATER
Kan sui (C)

Stores well, but being corrosive, store it in a bottle with a cork or glass stopper. Available from Chinese grocery stores.

ALMONDS
Hung yan (C)
杏仁

If shelled almonds are used, blanch and skin them first. Shelled and skinned almonds need no preparation.

ANGLED LOOFAH
Ketola (M)
See kua (C)
絲瓜

A dark green gourd of about 10 inches (25 cms) length with 10 angular ridges down its whole length. The flesh is soft and white.

ASAM GELUGOR
Asam pei (C)
亞三皮

Dried tamarind slices. If not available, use tamarind pulp instead. Available from Oriental food stores.

BAMBOO SHOOT
Rebong (M)
Choke so-un (C)
竹筍

The young shoot of the bamboo. Fresh bamboo shoot must be boiled for at least 1 hour to soften it before it can be used. After boiling, soak it in water till required. Boiled and ready-to-use bamboo shoot is available in cans from Oriental food stores.

BEAN CURD
Towfoo (C)
豆腐
Sui towfoo
水豆腐

Tow yuin
生花豆腐

Pak towfoo
白豆腐

Tow kon
豆乾
Yow chou towfoo
油炸豆腐
Towfoo pok
油炸豆腐球

Made from ground soy beans, it is sold in many forms. It has a delicate flavour and keeps fairly well in a refrigerator for up to a week, if it is immersed in water.
The softest and smoothest is made in 2 feet (60 cms) square slabs about 2 inches (5 cms) thick or in little boxes and sealed. This has the texture of baked custard.
Soft bean curd squares are a little firmer and are usually about 3 inches (8 cms) square 1 inch (2½ cms) thick. This is slightly firmer than the kind above. Handle carefully to prevent breaking it.
These firm bean curd squares are much easier to handle but are not as smooth textured as those above.
Very firm squares of about 3½ inches (9 cms) square and ¼ (1 cm) inch thick. These pieces of bean curd are sometimes coloured yellow.
Fried bean curd squares are fried till brown on the outside and honey-combed on the inside.
Fried bean curd balls are about 1 inch (2½ cms) in diameter and similar to the fried bean curd squares in texture.
Some, if not all these types of bean curd are available from Chinese food stores or Supermarkets.

BEAN-SPROUTS
Towgeh (M)
Ngah choy (C)
芽菜

Germinated green peas or green *mung* beans. Can be eaten uncooked in a salad or very lightly cooked as a vegetable. Use only the fresh variety which is tender and tasty. The canned variety is not recommended as it is soft and soggy. Fresh bean sprouts can be kept 3 to 4 days in a plastic bag in the refrigerator, or immersed in water to which a little salt has been added in a plastic container with a tight-fitting lid. Change the water daily. Available from Chinese food stores or supermarkets.

BLACAN
Ma lai chan (C)
馬來棧

Shrimp paste used widely in Southeast Asian recipes. It is available in rectangular cakes, flat round slabs or in cans. Its colour, depending on the variety and quality, ranges from pink to dark brown. It has a strong smell and should be kept in a tightly closed non-corrosive container. It keeps very well.

BUNGA KANTAN
Lam keong fah (C)
藍薑花

The pink, flower buds of a variety of ginger that looks very similar to the galingale plant. It is used as a flavouring in many dishes, especially fish curries.

CANDLENUT
Buah keras (M)
Saik ku chai (C)
石古仔

The oily kernel of a round nut, about 1¼ inches (3 cms) in diameter, with a very hard furrowed shell. The kernel looks very much like the macadamia nut and is used to thicken and enrich curries. If unavailable, use Brazil nuts, or macadamia nuts as substitute.

CAPSICUM
Tung loong chew (C)
燈籠椒

Also known as bell pepper. A large green, non-pungent fruit of about 3 inches (8 cms) diameter with thick, sweet flesh.

CASHEW-NUT
Yew tow (C)
腰豆

A kidney-shaped white nut with a sweet flavour that is available raw or roasted and salted.

CEKOR
sar keong (C)
沙薑

A miniature member of the ginger family with leaves not more than 4 inches (10 cms) long and the rhizomes less than 1 inch (2½ cms) long. It has a very pronounced aromatic flavour. It is available fresh from market stalls selling home produce. Chinese medicine shops sell the dried version which is in round slices.

CHILLIES
辣椒

Green and red ones are available, the red ones being normally hotter than the green. Red chillies are pounded or ground into a paste, chopped or used whole for flavouring, or cut in different ways for garnishing. Green chillies are usually used whole for flavouring, and cut differently for garnishing. Both red and green chillies can be pickled. Dried chillies are only used for flavouring.

CHILLI POWDER
辣椒粉

The powder obtained when dried chillies are ground. It is one of the main spices in curry powder.

CHILLI SAUCE
辣椒醬

Made from fresh red chillies with a touch of garlic to pep it up and salt, sugar and vinegar as preservatives and flavouring. The sauce has a blend of hot, sweet, sour and salt flavours carefully balanced.

CHINESE SAUSAGES
Lap cheong (C)
臘腸

Seasoned lean meat and pork fat are used to make Chinese sausages which are then dried in the sun so that they can keep even without refrigeration. To cook, either steam or fry them. They

134

are available from Chinese groceries and are sold loose or in cans.

CHINESE MUSHROOMS
Cendawan (M)
Toong ku/fah ku (C)
冬菇或花菇

They are dried and are either black in colour or are a very dark brown with white markings. Good quality mushrooms are evenly sized and are thick. These mushrooms have a flavour that is very distinct from any other mushrooms.

CHINESE SPINACH
Tong hoe (C)
茼蒿

A green, leafy, soft-stemmed vegetable with a very distinctive flavour. A very tender vegetable that is best lightly stir-fried or boiled.

CHINESE WHITE CABBAGE
Wong Ah Bak (C)
黃牙白

Looks like cos lettuce except that it is white in colour. The leaves are toothed, long and clasped tightly together.

CHINESE WINE
Siew Chow (C)
紹酒

A very old and mature rice wine that has changed to a reddish colour with age. It has a richer flavour than rice wine which is white.

CHIVES
Kuchai (M)
Kow choy (C)
韮菜

A small onion-like plant with long, narrow, flat leaves. It is best eaten raw or very lightly cooked. The yellow variety, called *Kow Wong* in Chinese, is a vegetable that is much sought after.

CHOCHO
Labu Siam (M)
Futt sow kua (C)
佛手瓜

Pale green, pear-shaped fruits with soft spines of a climbing plant. The young fruit is a delicious vegetable either boiled or stir-fried.

CINNAMON
Kayu manis (M)
Yoke kwai pei (C)
玉桂皮

The dried bark of the cinnamon tree is available as cinnamon sticks or ground cinnamon. Ground cinnamon loses its flavour if kept for too long, but the sticks will keep indefinitely. Obtainable from Chinese groceries, supermarkets, or Chinese medicine shops.

CLOVES
Bunga cingkeh (M)
Ting heong (C)
丁香

The little brown, dried flower buds that are so commonly used in cookery all over the world.

COCONUT MILK
Santan (M)
Yea cheong (C)
椰漿

The white, creamy liquid extracted from the grated flesh of fresh matured coconuts, used to flavour and enrich food.

CORIANDER
Ketumbar (M)
Yim sai mai (C)
芫茜米

The dried, brown seeds of the coriander plant is one of the main ingredients in curry powder. It is not hot but is very fragrant.

CORIANDER LEAVES
Daun ketumbar (M)
Yim sai (C)
芫茜

The young leaves of the coriander seedlings that is used in much the same way parsley is. In fact it is sometimes called Chinese parsley. Commonly used as a flavouring in soups and broths and as a garnishing.

CRAB MEAT
Hai yoke (C)
蟹肉

Available in cans or frozen. If fresh crabs are available, remove the pincers and shell and clean away all the fingers and intestines. Scrub them clean and steam them for ½ hour. When crabs are cooked, they turn a bright red. Cool them and the flesh can be separated from the shell quite easily. A kilo of fresh crabs of good quality should give about 1½ to 2 cups crabmeat. Crabmeat stores well in a freezer.

CUMIN
Jintan putih (M)
Sai kook (C)
細殼

Another ingredient in curry powder.

CURRY LEAVES
Karupillai (M)
Kali yip (C)
咖喱葉

Small, dark green, shiny leaves, strongly flavoured and mainly used in Indian curries. Available fresh or dried from Oriental food stores.

CURRY POWDER
咖喱粉

Best to grind one's own if it is used in quantity. For those who use a little occasionally, it is best to buy the prepared brands as curry powder deteriorates with keeping. Many different brands are now available; try them out and decide on which brand suits your taste best. Always buy in small quantities and use them as fresh as possible. Available from Oriental food stores.

DAUN KADEOK
Gar lowe (C)
假桍葉

A shiny, club-shaped leaf from a weak stemmed plant that grows wild in the tropics. It grows along the side of many roads and is like a weed in many gardens. Its peculiar flavour is not acceptable to many people.

DAUN KESSOM
辣柳葉

A little plant that rarely grows taller than 10 inches (25 cms) with pointed, thin and narrow leaves of about 1½ inches (4 cms) long and ½ inch (1 cm) wide. It is used for flavouring Laksa gravies and a few special dishes.

DAUN LIMAU PERUT
Fatt foong kum yip (C)
發瘋柑葉

The young leaves of a rough-skinned lime. The leaves are often pounded with *sambal blacan* to give it a lemony flavour. It can be shredded or added whole to flavour curries. The fruit is not used for cooking but is used as a hair rinse.

DRIED OYSTERS
Hoe see/tam choy
乾蠔／淡菜

They come in different sizes. The large ones of about 1½ inches (4 cms) length are very expensive. Dried oysters must be soaked for a couple of hours to soften them before they can be cleansed of all grit and sand. They are available from Chinese groceries.

DRIED PRAWNS
Udang kering (M)
Har mai (C)
蝦米

Sun-dried steamed prawns. Soak them for about 20 minutes and they can be used in place of fresh prawns though the flavour is different.

EGGPLANTS, BRINJALS or AUBERGINES
Terong (M)
Ngai kwa (C)
矮瓜

There is the egg-shaped variety and the oblong variety. Both varieties have the white fruits or the deep purple fruits. The latter have a slightly tougher skin but all have the same flavour.

FENNEL
Jintan manis (M)
Tai kook (C)
大殼

Looks very much like cumin except that it is a larger grain. It also has a stronger flavour, so it must be used with care.

FENUGREEK
Alba (M)
胡蘆巴籽

These little, flat, squarish, brown seeds are used mainly for fish curries. They have a bitter flavour and are best used whole and not ground. Fry them lightly in the oil before adding in the curry paste.

FISH SAUCE
Yu loe (C)
魚露

A light brown, thin sauce very much like the poor quality light soy sauce. When smelt, it has a slight fishy smell, but when used to flavour food it gives a better flavour than soy sauce and the fishy flavour is not noticed. The poor grades of fish sauce are very salty and must be used with care to make sure food is not over-seasoned. Available from supermarkets or Chinese groceries.

FIVE-SPICE POWDER
Ng heong fun (C)
五香粉

A brown powder made from mixed spices. It is obtainable from Chinese medicine shops, or Oriental food stores.

FRIED EGG NOODLES
伊 麵

Look under Noodles.

FRIED *TOWFOO* BALLS
油炸豆腐球

Look under Bean Curd.

FU PEI
腐皮

Bean curd skins are thin, yellow pieces of skin from the top of soy bean milk before it coagulates. They are paper-thin and are about 2 feet (60 cms) square or round. They are sold folded like plastic sheets from stalls selling bean curd, Chinese groceries and supermarkets.

GALINGALE
Lengkuas (M)
Larm keong (C)
藍薑

A rhizome of the ginger family that is a very popular flavouring used in Malaysian cookery. It has a shiny off-white skin with brown markings. The white flesh is fairly hard and fibrous. It can be sliced, dried and stored.

GARLIC
Bawang putih (M)
Suin tow (C)
蒜頭

Available in two varieties, the brown skinned variety and the white skinned variety. Used very extensively as a flavouring.

GHEE
印度酥油

This is clarified butter and is therefore pure butter fat. It gives food a rich and distinctive flavour. Sold in tins in Oriental food stores.

GINGERLY SEEDS or SESAME SEEDS
Bijan (M)
Chi-mah (C)
芝蔴

These very tiny, white seeds shaped like tear-drops are normally washed and dry-fried or roasted in a frying pan till they are lightly browned. When cool they are stored, to be used when required. They are sprinkled on cooked food as a flavouring.

GINGER
Halia (M)
Keong (C)
薑

Fresh root ginger is used as a flavouring for all seafoods and all poultry dishes. It is quite common to find many people using ginger in all their food because of its mildly pungent flavour. If fresh ginger is not available, use ground ginger.

GLUTEN BALLS
Mien kun (C)
麵根

Brown, light, round balls of deep-fried wheat gluten. They keep very well in the freezer. Scald them just before using and squeeze out all the water. This is used mainly for vegetarian dishes. Available from Chinese groceries.

GREEN PEA FLOUR or MUNG BEAN FLOUR
Tepong Hoen Kwe (M)
Look tow fun (C)
六豆粉

Obtained from ground green peas or *mung* beans, this flour is used to give Malaysian *Kuih* an elastic texture that is not tough. A custard made with this flour has a more springy texture that is very acceptable. Transparent noodles is made from this flour. Available in packed rolls of about 1 cup flour from Chinese groceries and supermarkets. The pure flour is sold loose in Bangkok, Medan and Penang.

GROUPER
Kerapu (M)
Sek pan (C)
石斑魚

A tropical fish found from the estuaries to the deep waters and usually in the vicinity of rock and coral reefs. A good fish for the table because of its tender and fine-textured flesh. Trout makes a good substitute.

GULA MELAKA
Yea tong (C)
椰糖

Cakes of dark brown sugar made from the sap of the coconut palm. Good quality gula melaka has a very strong flavour of coconut.

HOI SUIN SAUCE
海鮮醬

A very thick sweet, red sauce. It looks very much like tomato paste. It is used to marinate certain foods, as well as an accompanying sauce to be served at table. Available in bottles or tins from Oriental food stores, Chinese groceries or supermarkets.

IKAN BILIS
Kong yu chai (C)
江魚仔

Dried anchovies. Remove the head and intestines, rinse quickly and dry thoroughly before storing. Keeps very well. Fry them in deep-fat when they are dry and they make delicious, crisp tit-bits for cocktails. Available from Oriental food stores and Chinese groceries.

LEMON GRASS
Serai (M)
Heong mow (C)
香茅

A tall grass with very fleshy leaf-bases that are used for flavouring food, especially curries. Use only 4 inches (10 cms) to 5 inches (12 cms) of the slightly swollen leaf-bases. When sliced and dried, they keep very well. Fresh ones are available from Oriental food stores at certain times.

LONG BEANS
Kacang Panjang (M)
Tow kok (C)
豆角

Sometimes known as string beans. Each bean measures 15 to 20 inches (37½ to 50 cms) and is about ¼ inch (½ cm) to ½ inch (1 cm) in diameter.

LOTUS SEEDS
Lin chee (C)
蓮子

Dried lotus seeds are round, brown-coloured seeds of about ½ inch (1 cm) diameter. They need to be soaked and boiled to soften them so that the skin can be removed. The green germ in the centre must also be removed as it is bitter. Cleaned and ready-to-cook lotus seeds are available from some supermarkets. The dried ones are available from Chinese groceries or medicine shops.

MACKERAL
Ikan kembong (M)
Kamong yu (C)
甘望魚

This fish is available in most countries.

MEEHOON 米粉	Look under Noodles.
MINT *Daun pudina* (M) *Pok ho/Heong fah choy* (C) 薄荷葉　香花菜	Used mainly for Laksa.
MOK YEE (wood-ear fungus) 木耳	A fungus that is found on rotting wood. This looks like elephant's ears and is black on one side and a light brownish-white on the underside. Available from Chinese groceries and Oriental food stores.
MONOSODIUM GLUTAMATE *Mei ching* (C) 味精	Best known under the brand names "Aji-no-moto" and "Vetsin". Used mainly to improve the flavour of food. Home cooked dishes using sufficient good quality ingredients and which have been carefully seasoned do not need this seasoning.
MUSSELS *Lah-lah* (C)	Buy only those that are still alive as it is unhealthy to eat them unless they are absolutely fresh.
MUSTARD GREEN *Sayor sawi* (M) *Choy sum* (C) 菜心	Plants of about 12 inches (30 cms) tall with long, green leaf-stalks surmounted with round-bladed dark green leaves. When old, they have yellow flowers at the shoot.
MUSTARD SEEDS *Biji sawi* (M) 芥蘭菜	Tiny, bead-like, black seeds used to flavour curries and pickles.
MYSENTERY *Ju mong yow* (C) 猪網油	The lacy layer of fat from around the pig's stomach that is used to wrap up food for deep-fat frying. Order from the butcher.
NOODLES *Darn mien* (C) 蛋麵 *Mien kon* (C) 麵乾	Egg noodles are available in both thick and thin strands, coiled into little heaps. They are available from the market or supermarket. Dried egg noodles are available from Chinese groceries, supermarkets and food emporiums. They are yellow-coloured noodles either in round cakes of about 2½ inches (6½ cms) diameter, or rectangular pieces of about 3 inches (7½ cms) square. Some are also sold in straight sticks very much like spaghetti, in boxes.
Yee mien (C) 伊麵	Fried egg noodles are loosely packed, round pieces of yellowish, pinkish noodles. They are very crisp and break easily.
Meehoon (M) *Mei fun* (C) 米粉	Rice vermicelli is thin, white strands of dried noodles. They are sometimes known as rice noodles.
Hokkien mee (M) *Fukien mien* (C) 福建麵	Yellow noodles are always sold fresh. They are a bright yellow colour and are coated very lightly with oil to prevent them sticking to each other and to give them a slight sheen. They are available in thick and thin strands

139

Sohoon (M)
Fun see (C)
粉絲

Transparent noodles are thin, dried, white noodles made from green pea flour. They are sometimes called bean thread or Chinese vermicelli.
All dried noodles are available from Chinese groceries, Food emporiums, or supermarkets. Fresh noodles are available from supermarkets or markets.

ONIONS
Bawang (M)
Choong tow (C)
洋葱頭

The most common are the red-skinned and the brown-skinned varieties. The red-skinned variety has a "sharper" flavour and the brown-skinned variety is sweeter.

OYSTER SAUCE
Ho yow (C)
蠔油

A thick, brown sauce with a delicate flavour of oysters. Available from Chinese groceries and supermarkets.

PANDANUS or SCREWPINE
Daun pandan (M)
Lum pei yip (C)
香葉

Stiff, long and narrow, bright green leaves with a pronounced furrow down its centre. When cooked with food, it gives food a lovely flavour. The leaves are pounded and the green juice extracted to be added to food for colouring as well as flavouring.

PAPAYA
Mok kua (C)
木瓜

Also known as pawpaw. The raw fruit has crisp, firm flesh which can be pickled. When it ripens, the flesh becomes soft and sweet.

PEPPERCORNS
Lada (M)
Woo chew lup (C)
胡椒粒

Available in white and black. White peppercorns are more commonly used.

PLUM SAUCE
Suin mui cheong (C)
酸梅醬

A spicy, sweet sauce of a golden colour with shredded chillies in it. Available in bottles from Chinese groceries and supermarkets.

POMFRET
Bawal (M)
Chong Yu (C) 鯧魚

There are three species of pomfrets, which are called Stromateus or Rudderfish in some countries. A good substitute for this delicate fish is the Turbot.

Bawal tambah (M)
Tau tai chong (C) 兜底鯧

The best species for eating as it has very tender, delicately flavoured flesh. It is coloured more greyish than silvery and the fins are greyish black.

Bawal putih (M)
Pak chong (C) 白鯧

A silvery-white fish that does not have as thick flesh as the *bawal tambah*, but is otherwise just as good.

Bawal hitam (M)
Huk chong (C) 黑鯧

A deep grey-coloured fish that is not as tasty as the other two species. This fish can be very good for curries or other more highly spiced dishes.

POPPY SEEDS
Kas-kas
罌粟籽

Usually ground and added to curry powder to improve flavour as well as to enrich and thicken it.

PRESERVED CABBAGE
Tong choy (C)
冬菜

Available loose from Chinese groceries, square pieces of golden brown cabbage leaves pre-served and packed into squat, round, glazed, brown earthern-jars.

PRESERVED RADISH
Tai tou choy (C)
大頭菜

Two types are available.
The whole radish is cut into slices lengthwise and with all the leaves intact is salted and dried.

Choy poh (C) 菜脯	The cleaned and skinned radish is cut into even-sized pieces and is preserved with spices and salt to get golden brown pieces that are crisp and delicious eaten as a relish. Both types are available from Chinese groceries.
PRESERVED MUSTARD GREEN 　*Mui choy* (C) 　梅菜	Whole plants of mustard greens are salted until they become very limp before they are dried.
PUCHOK 　*Fuchok* (C) 　腐竹	Crisp yellow pieces of dried beancurd skin that are sometimes called beancurd sticks.
PULUT (M) 　*Loh mei* (C) 　糯米	A short-grained rice that is very starchy and sticky when cooked, for which reason it is sometimes called glutinous rice.
RADISH 　*Lobak* (M) 　*Lobak* (C) 　蘿蔔	This is more commonly known as Chinese radish. It is a long, white, cylindrical root that measures from 8 inches (20 cms) to about 18 inches (45 cms) long.
RICE FLOUR 　*Chim mei fun* (C) 　粘米粉	A very white, granular flour sold in packets in most groceries and supermarkets.
RICE FLOUR-DAMP 　*Chim mei fun* (C) 　濕粘米粉	Fresh, ground rice flour that is used for Malaysian *kuih-kuih*. The dried flour does not give as good a flavour as the fresh, ground flour.
RICE WINE 　*Mei chou* (C) 　米酒	A white wine fermented from rice. Available in both large and small bottles from Chinese groceries and supermarkets.
ROCK SALT 　*Cho yim* (C) 　粗鹽	Grey crystals of rock salt are normally used for preservation.
ROCK SUGAR 　*Ping tong* (C) 　冰糖	Large lumps of sugar crystals that are sweeter than granulated sugar.
SAGO 　*Sar kok mai* (C) 　沙谷米	Sago used in this book is actually pearl sago, which is manufactured from sago flour obtained from the pith of the sago palm. Sago is obtainable from Chinese groceries and supermarkets.
SAYOR MANIS 　*Su chai choy* (C) 　樹仔菜	A small plant that is often planted as a low hedge around farm gardens. The young leaves and shoots make a very good vegetable.
SESAME OIL or GINGELLY OIL 　*Mah yow* (C) 　蔴油	A rather dark-coloured oil that is used for flavouring and not for cooking. Sold in bottles in Chinese groceries and supermarkets.

SHALLOTS
Bawang merah (M)
Choong tow chai (C)
葱頭仔

Small, purplish onions with reddish-brown skins that grow in clusters and so are seldom round like onions. The smaller ones with the more reddish skins are "sharper" in flavour.

SHARK'S FINS
Yu chee (C)
魚鰭

Whole dried fins require hours of preparation to extract the edible jelly-like needles.
Cleaned shark's fins are available from Chinese or Oriental food stores.

SNOW PEAS, GARDEN PEAS or SUGAR PEAS
Hollan dow (C)
荷蘭豆

Green peas in the pod that need very little cooking and are very tender.

SOY SAUCE
Sang chow (C) — light
醬青／生抽
Huk yow (C) — dark
黑油

There is the light sauce and the dark. The former is normally used for flavouring, while the dark sauce is used not only for flavouring but also to give colour. Available from most Chinese or Oriental food stores.

SPINACH
Bayam (M)
Yin choy (C)
莧菜

Can be substituted with kangkong or lettuce.

SPRING ONION
Daun bawang (M)
Choong (C)
生葱

the round, hollow leaves of the onion which are used as a vegetable, as a garnishing or for flavouring.

STAR ANISE
Bunga lawang (M)
Paht kok (C)
八角

This star-shaped seed and seed-pod is used as a flavouring. It is more often used whole and removed after cooking.

SWEET BEAN PASTE
Tow sar (C)
豆沙

Made from red peas and used as a filling for some sweet dishes.

SWEET POTATO
Ubi keledek (M)
Farm su (C)
蕃薯

They can have flesh that is white, cream, orange or purplish-blue in colour.

SWEET POTATO GREENS
Farn su mew (C)
蕃薯苗

The young leaves and shoots of the sweet potato creeper. Spinach is a good substitute.

SZECHUAN PEPPER
Fah chew (C)
花椒

Little, brown, dried berries about the size of coriander seeds. They are reddish-brown in colour and are available from Chinese medicine shops.

SZECHUAN VEGETABLE
Char choy (C)
炸菜

Preserved heart of the mustard cabbage. It is very spicy. Available from Chinese groceries.

142

TAMARIND
Assam (M)
Asam koh (C)
亞三哥

The brown pulp and black seeds of the assam fruit is used to give a sour taste to food. It is sold in packets. The brown — coloured tamarind is fresher than the black.

TAPIOCA
Ubi kayu (M)
Mook su (C)
木薯

The starchy, swollen roots of the tapioca plant. The flesh under the brown skin is very white.

TAPIOCA FLOUR
Su fun (C)
薯粉

Obtained by grating and drying tapioca and reducing it to flour by grinding. It has similar properties to cornflour.

TEEMCHOK
甜竹

Seasoned, brown rectangular pieces of dried soy bean curd used mainly in vegetarian cookery.

TEEM CHEONG
甜醬

Look under Hoi Suin sauce.

THREADFIN
Ikan kurau (M)
Mah yow yu or
mah yow chai (C)
馬友魚或馬友仔

A good but expensive fish. A good substitute is the snapper.

TUMERIC
Kunyit (M)
Wong keong (C)
黃薑

A rhizome of the ginger family with bright orange-yellow flesh that is used in most curries and pickles. If fresh tumeric is not available, use the dried or ground type.

TOWCHEONG
Mien see (C)
豆醬

Soy bean paste used to flavour food, or to make certain sauces.

VEGETABLE MARROW
Kundor (M)
Chit kwa (C)
節瓜

A fleshy fruit with a "hairy" skin. It is light or dark green in colour.

WOLF HERRING
Ikan parang (M)
Sai toh yu (C)
西刀魚

A well-flavoured fish that is very bony.

WATER CHESTNUTS
mah tai (C)
馬蹄

Corms with brownish-black skins and white flesh. The flesh is sweet and crispy. It is available fresh, which means the skin has to be washed and peeled, or in tins. Substitute with yam beans if not available.

WATERCRESS
Sai yeong choy (C)
西洋菜

Usually boiled or stir-fried and hardly ever eaten raw.

WATER CONVOLVULUS
Kangkong (M)
Ung choy (C)
甕菜

A green leafy vegetable that grows beside streams.

WONTON SKIN
  Wonton pei (C)
  雲吞皮

Paper-thin 3 inch (7½ cms) squares of egg noodle dough. Available wherever fresh egg noodle is available.

YAMS
  Keladi (M)
  Woo tow (C)
  芋頭

A purplish-red root that has a slightly furry brown skin.

YAM BEAN
  Bangkuang/sengkuang (M)
  Sar gott (C)
  沙葛

This tuberous root has a brown skin that can be peeled away from the white flesh which is sweet.

Spices

1. *Assam gelugur* - dried tamarind slices
2. *Blacan* - prawn paste pressed into cakes.
3. *Buah keras* - candlenut. A round nut with a hard, black shell. The white, oily kernel is used to enrich curries and *sambals*.
4. *Bunga kantan* - pink flower bud of the galingale.
5. Candlenut - see *buah keras*.
6. Cardamom - *buah pelaga*. Dried seeds of the cardamom plant. Usually bought whole in the grey-white pod.
7. *Cekor* - a small plant of the ginger family. Both the leaves and the rhizomes are used for flavouring.
8. Chillies - bright red fruit of the chilli plant. Some varieties are very pungent. Green chillies are normally milder in flavour. Used mainly in curries and *sambals* to give the pungent flavour. Makes very attractive garnishes. Dried chillies give food a duller red colour.
9. Cinnamon - *kayu manis*. The fragrant bark of the cinnamon tree.
10. Cloves - *bunga cingkeh*. The dried flower buds of a species of myrtle.
11. Coriander leaves - young plants from seeds used for seasoning and garnishing. Sometimes called Chinese parsley.
12. Curry leaves - Strongly flavoured leaves used mainly for Indian curries.
13. *Daun kadeok* - a weed with leaves similar to betel leaves.
14. *Daun Kessom* - small plant with spear-shaped leaves.
15. *Daun kunyit* - leaf of the tumeric plant.
16. *Daun limau perut* - leaves of a tree which is a member of the lime family. The fruits have dark-green, knobly skins.
17. *Daun pandan* - see pandan leaves.
18. dried peel - dark-brown dried skin of mandarin oranges or tangerines.
19. *Fah Chew* - Szechuan pepper or allspice. Looks similar to black pepper. When crushed, it has the smell of nutmeg.
20. Garlic - a dried bulb that is made up of a number of individual sections called cloves. It has a very strong and penetrating smell and flavour.
21. Ginger - the rhizome of a tropical plant with a pungent taste. Old ginger is used for extracting ginger juice while the young sections are more often used sliced or shredded.
22. *Halba* - Fenugreek or Greek Hay.
23. *Jintan manis* - Aniseed or anise. It is the seed from a plant which is a member of the magnolia family.
24. *Jintan putih* - Cummin. It is the seed of the cummin plant which is a member of the parsley family. The seeds look and taste like caraway.
25. *Kas-kas* - dry poppy seeds.
26. *Ketumbar* - coriander seeds. Dried seeds of a plant similar to parsley.
27. *Lengkuas* - galingale. Use the young rhizomes sparingly.

28.	Lemon grass	-	*serai*. The fleshy leaf-base and the stem of a fragrant grass.
29.	Mustard seeds	-	small, brownish-black seeds of the mustard plant.
30.	*Pandan* leaves (Screwpine leaves)	-	long, narrow leaves of the *pandan* plant that is used for colouring and flavouring.
31.	Shallots	-	a cluster of two or more red-coloured bulbs which are rarely rounded.
32.	Star anise	-	star-shaped, dry seeds in their pods.
33.	Tamarind	-	pulp from the seed pods of the tamarind tree. The pulp is a golden brown colour mixed with seeds when fresh. Black coloured tamarind has been kept a long time and is not as good as the fresh, lighter coloured type.
34.	Turmeric	-	fresh or dried rhizomes of a plant similar to ginger. When mature, the rhizomes have a deep yellow colour.